The Power of Positive Teaching

35 Successful Strategies for Active and Enthusiastic Classroom Participation

Yvonne Bender

nomad press

Also by Yvonne Bender:

The New Teacher's Handbook: Practical Strategies & Techniques for Success in the Classroom from Kindergarten Through High School

Nomad Press
A division of Nomad Communications
10 9 8 7 6 5 4 3 2

ISBN: 0-9722026-9-2

Questions regarding the ordering of this book should be addressed to
Independent Publishers Group
814 N. Franklin St.
Chicago, IL 60610
www.ipgbook.com

Nomad Press
2456 Christian St.
White River Junction, VT 05001
www.nomadpress.net

To the many teachers who strive daily to make a positive difference in the lives of their students.

Acknowledgements

I wish to gratefully acknowledge the following people for their assistance in writing *The Power of Positive Teaching:*

Melanie Gaieski for the many hours spent reading, reviewing, and offering advice on content and style.

Lauri Berkenkamp for frequent encouragement and excellent editing skills.

Charlotte Davis for constant support and faithful friendship.

Mary Ellen Ericson for review of content and objective feedback.

Table of Contents

Part III—*Let's Get It All Together*

Strategies That Keep Students Organized...............61

Part IV—*Positively Perfect*

Strategies That Build Self-Esteem and
Create a Positive Learning Environment 89

Introduction

One of the most difficult tasks teachers face is that of consistently creating an active, joyful, and educationally productive learning environment. *The Power of Positive Teaching* contains thirty-five practical and easy strategies to help you meet that challenge. Gleaned during my thirty-year teaching career and implemented successfully with scores of students of all grade and ability levels, the strategies in *The Power of Positive Teaching* are classroom tested and actually do create positive student attitudes and productive learning environments.

Every strategy can easily be modified to meet the unique educational, social, and emotional needs of your students, your preferred teaching style, and the behavioral guidelines set by your school. Each strategy is explained in an easy-to-follow, concise (two-to-three page), point-by-point format that includes the following:

- A brief introductory scenario illustrating the usefulness of the approach in the classroom.

- Statements categorizing the strategy and delineating its goal(s).

- An explanation of how the technique accomplishes its goal(s).

- Steps to implement the strategy.

- A discussion of potential problems that using the approach might cause and suggestions for managing them.

- Viable ideas for adapting the techniques to fit different teaching situations.

It is my hope that the strategies in *The Power of Positive Teaching* will not only save you hours of planning consternation, but more importantly, bring much joy of learning to your classroom.

Part I

Your Attention, Please!

Strategies That Gain and Keep Students' Attention

 Inside Part I

- Focused Finale
- Teacher's Helper
- Highly Focused, Graded Test Review
- Student Created Test
- Have the Last Word When Reading
- Hands Down, Ears Open
- Build a Break
- Playing Card Pick
- Beach Party
- Basketball Free Throw Review
- Who Wants to Be a Millionaire?

My Journey From Teaching Frustration to Teaching Fulfillment

Never has the adage "necessity is the mother of invention" proven more true than when I first implemented the strategies explained in *Your Attention, Please!* Assigned to teach a class of exceptionally bright, yet seriously emotionally disturbed students with attention deficit (ADD) and attention deficit hyperactivity (ADHD) disorders, my major concern was how to form educationally conducive order from dysfunctional, counterproductive chaos. Since I was a starving young teacher desperately in need of her job, I was motivated by a very strong desire to succeed and searched for ways to gain control of—and ultimately teach—my very active and highly distractible students.

After several weeks of exasperating failure, I had a small glimmer of hope late one day, when out of sheer frustration, I simply began calling on students at random. I didn't wait for them to volunteer, but just called out a name and asked a question. After the first few questions I found myself using a rapid-fire, auctioneer style (hamming it up a bit as I went). Miracle of miracles, it worked! My students began focusing on the lesson and, for the moment, stopped annoying one another.

After using this fast-paced, question-and-answer teaching style with relatively positive results for a few days, I started adding other game-type activities to my teaching arsenal. I knew that my students' attention tended to dwindle toward the end of class and came up with *Focused Finale, Build a Break,* and *Who Wants to be a Millionaire?.* For those times when they were just itching for movement, there was *Beach Party, Playing Card Pick,* the *Basketball Free Throw Review.* None of my creative endeavors were necessarily earth shattering, but each of them helped keep my students focused and learning, and helped me become a successful teacher.

A Word About *Your Attention, Please!*

Teachers have always faced competition for their students' attention. Everything from peer pressure and family conflicts to neighborhood dynamics can cause students to lose focus on the lesson at hand. Today's technology-savvy students, however, pose even greater challenges for their teachers. Raised in the age of computerized electronic technology, with its instant access to information and rapid-fire verbal and visual feedback, these students often find their schoolwork, with its requisite slower-paced, review-oriented presentations, tedious and boring.

Instead of admonishing a class with, "I keep seeing the same hands over and over. How about someone else volunteering to answer this question?" you need a strategy that compels nonparticipants to focus and participate. Instead of spending hours meticulously grading test papers only to have your students give them a cursory glance, crumple them into a ball, and throw them in the trash, you need a technique that encourages them to focus on and learn from their mistakes.

Your Attention, Please! provides useful strategies and techniques that will draw your students into a lesson and compel them to focus and attend throughout. While some, such as *Highly Focused Graded Test Review* and *Have The Last Word When Reading*, are useful with specific kinds of lessons, others, such as *Focused Finale* and *Hands Down Ears Open*, have more general applications. All of the strategies, however, are highly versatile, lend well to adaptation, and will help you gain and maintain your students' attention and interest.

Focused Finale

It is near the end of an introductory geometry class and the teacher announces, "All right, everyone, listen up. It's time for your ticket-to-dismissal challenge questions."

There is a pause in the class as students who are surreptitiously starting to pack up their materials for the next class stop to listen.

"Today there are three questions," the teacher continues. He then presents the questions to the class and calls on students to answer them. As each question is answered, the teacher playfully reminds the students how many remaining questions they must answer before they can be dismissed. When the final question is answered correctly, the class breaks into cheers and the lesson ends in a positive and productive fashion.

What It Is: *Focused Finale* is a strategy that challenges a class to answer two or three pivotal review questions as their ticket for dismissal. It helps keep students focused during the end-of-lesson review.

Why It's Used: "Good teaching practice" calls for an end-of-lesson review to help students retain the lesson's most important points. Students, however, are often more focused on preparing for the next lesson or gathering up their belongings to move to the next class than they are in the transpiring review. (This is perfectly normal behavior. Just think of your own and your colleagues' behavior at the end of a faculty meeting or workshop!) The challenge is to find a way to hold your students' attention until the lesson actually concludes.

How It's Done: At least five minutes before the end of the lesson, in a good-natured, nonthreatening manner, introduce the conditions necessary for dismissal. *Focused Finale* should be seen as an affable and achievable challenge, not an adversarial provocation. For example, you might say something like: During today's lesson we covered some important new information. Before I dismiss you, I need to be sure that you understand what was covered, so as your ticket out of here, I need someone to tell me:

1. What is a right triangle?

2. Why is it useful to know that a triangle is a right triangle?

3. How many acute or obtuse angles can a right triangle have?

The first time you use this technique it is acceptable to call on students whom you feel sure can answer correctly. It is unacceptable and undermines the technique's effectiveness, however, to call on these same students at the end of every class.

(**Perils and Pitfalls:**) Students who resent authority figures can be surly and rebellious and make comments such as, "You can't keep me here past the bell. If I'm late for my next class, you'll have to write an excuse note for me!"

To avoid such unpleasant scenarios:

1. Introduce the *Focused Finale* in a low-key manner.

2. Allow more than enough time to cover the review questions the first few times you use this technique.

3. Ensure your students' success when introducing the *Focused Finale* by using easier-to-answer review questions and moving to more challenging types of questions once your students feel confident they can meet your challenge.

(**Variations on a Theme:**)

- Write the review questions on the board, a transparency, or computer display. Keep them hidden during class and challenge your students to formulate appropriate review questions for the day's lesson. Then dramatically reveal and compare your questions with theirs.

- Have your students write their names on slips of paper, place the slips in a hat, and each day have a student draw out the names of students to answer the finale questions. Continue drawing the names from the hat over the course of several days until every student has had a chance to answer. (When using this variation, do not reveal the review question until after a student's name is drawn so you can adjust the difficulty of your question to the ability level of the student who is expected to answer.)

- If you have divided your class into teams or work groups, select a team to answer the day's review questions and allow them to collaborate on the answer.

Sound Advice

No One Has an Answer,
Now What?

If your students get stuck and can't answer the Focused Finale *question, try these strategies to steer them toward an acceptable answer.*

You can:

- *Back up gently and ask an easier question that you are fairly certain almost everyone can answer. This is accomplished by making a conciliatory statement such as, "Before we tackle that question, who can tell us . . ."*

- *Draw blank lines on the chalkboard to correspond with the number of letters in a correct one-word answer or the correct number of words in a multiword answer and fill in some clue letters or words as necessary as in the style of Hang Man or Wheel of Fortune.*

- *Give your students oral clues beginning with the less obvious and moving toward the more obvious. You might say for instance, "We spoke about this person at the beginning of the lesson. He was a general in the Revolutionary War. You probably see his picture at least once every day, especially if you go shopping," and so forth.*

Teacher's Helper

It is the middle of a lesson and a teacher has paused to write an important point on the board. She looks for a piece of chalk but can't seem to find any. Suddenly a small boy seated near the front of the room jumps up and hands her the chalk.

"Good job, William." The teacher says quietly. "I don't know what I'd do if I didn't have a teaching assistant like you keeping track of things for me."

William, a child with attention deficit hyperactivity disorder, beams a huge smile of pride, takes his seat, and focuses on the teacher's every move.

(**What It Is:**) *Teacher's Helper* technique is a way to gain and retain a distractible student's attention and keep him or her from distracting others. It motivates the student to pay attention and prevents him or her from annoying others nearby.

(**Why It's Used:**) It provides a positive outlet for the overly active student's excess energy.

(**How It's Done:**)

1. Decide on a way the overly active student can be of assistance to you as you teach a lesson.

2. Talk with the student's parents and gain their permission to implement your plan.

3. Meet with the student and ask him for his help. Be sure to set specific behavioral guidelines. (See sample teacher–student dialogue.)

4. Move the student to an area of the classroom where he can assist you without disturbing others.

5. Reinforce the student's appropriately helpful behavior.

Sample Teacher–Student Dialogue

Teacher: I wanted to talk with you, William, because I'd like you to help me out.

(William looks puzzled but nods his head, 'yes.')

Teacher: I guess you've noticed that when I'm teaching, I have a terrible problem keeping track of my chalk and board erasers and stuff like that?

William: (Nodding his head) Yeah, I know! I never seen anybody lose chalk and erasers and junk the way you do, Mrs. M.

Teacher: I know, William, and that's why I need your help. Do you think, if I moved you closer to the front of the room, you could be my teaching assistant and help keep track of my materials for me?

William: (Confidently) Sure, I can do that, Mrs. M.

Teacher: Oh, I know you can keep track of my chalk and erasers and such, William, but can you find them and give them to me without disturbing the rest of the class and interrupting the lesson?

William: No problem, Mrs. M. I can help you keep track of all of your teaching stuff and nobody will even know I'm around.

Teacher: Okay, William, let's do this. Let's try having you be my teaching assistant for the next two days. Then, we'll meet and talk about how we're doing and see if we want to continue. What do you say? Do we have a deal?

William: Yeah, sure. Why not? Let's do it.

(Perils and Pitfalls:) Since overly helpful "teaching assistants" can be extremely distracting to the rest of the class, it is important that they be required to follow very specific behavioral guidelines based on the task that they are given and their unique behavioral needs.

Also, parents of a distractible student will sometimes complain about their child being the teacher's servant. Avoid such complaints by speaking with the parents before suggesting this program to the child. Explain the purpose for implementing the strategy and gain their permission to use it with their child.

In some classes, nondistractible students may become jealous and resentful of the special status granted to the distractible child. Prevent this jealousy by having the non-distractible students assist you with routine tasks (depending on your students' age and skill levels) such as washing the boards, delivering messages, marking the classroom calendar for special events, keeping the furniture organized, picking up the classroom, distributing and collecting papers, and so forth.

Variations on a Theme:

- Teachers with more than one seriously distractible student can have them alternate as assistants throughout the lesson.

- Consider using a temporary version of this technique by choosing an especially fidgety student to be your temporary personal helper for one class period only. For example, a temporary personal helper might hold a chart for the class while you teach part of the lesson or be responsible for pointing to specific vocabulary words on a chart as the class reviews them.

Highly Focused, Graded Test Review

A teacher is returning graded work to his students.

"I've marked your test papers and am returning them to you. When you get your paper, take a few minutes to review it and then leave it on your desk. You'll need to have it out because we're going to go over the answers together. As we do, I expect you to correct your mistakes by copying the correct answers under the incorrect answers. Be sure to make your corrections carefully because each corrected answer will add one point back to your final test grade."

A student near the back of the room raises his hand and asks, "Let me get this straight. You're going to give us the correct answers and if we copy them down, we get points added to our grade?"

"All you have to do is pay close attention and copy them down CORRECTLY, Josh," answers the teacher with a smile.

"No sweat!" Josh replies.

(What It Is:) *Highly Focused, Graded Test Review* is a procedure that compels students to focus closely on their test errors. It encourages students to carefully examine their teacher's feedback on tests and use it as a learning tool.

(Why It's Used:) It's not unusual for students, especially those who receive a poor grade on a test, simply to give the paper a cursory look, crumple it up, and toss it in the trash. This behavior is counterproductive to the student's learning process and frustrating to the teacher who has spent much time providing the student with individualized written feedback. *Highly Focused, Graded Test Review* addresses this problem by requiring students to focus on and correct their test errors, and rewarding them with improved test scores when they do so. It also assuages students' test-taking anxiety since they know that they will be given an opportunity to learn from and correct their mistakes after the test has been graded. This approach helps students master the material covered on the test.

(How It's Done:) Explain the *Highly Focused, Graded Test Review* procedure to your class (as in the above scenario) and implement it when needed.

(Perils and Pitfalls:) Since this procedure requires you to take additional time to review and regrade student-corrected papers, you may choose to implement it only when administering major unit tests or when test results indicate the majority of your students did not master the concepts evaluated by the test. Keep in mind, however, that the additional time given to reviewing and regrading is often well spent since it saves you time from reteaching concepts that can be quickly and easily clarified when you have your students' undivided attention during *Highly Focused, Graded Test Review.*

(Variations on a Theme:)

- After completing *Highly Focused, Graded-Test Review,* re-administer the same test and have students complete only those items missed on the original test or give students a mini-test consisting of two or three problems similar to those they missed on the original test.

Sound Advice

How Many Points to Give?

You must be sure to set a realistic point value for corrected test items. A value that is too high can cause marginal students to rely on Highly Focused, Graded Test Review *for improved test grades in lieu of good study habits, and a value that is too low won't motivate students during* Highly Focused, Graded Test Review. *The trick is to give enough point value to provide incentive for your students to carefully correct their test errors but not so much value that they view their initial test grades as insignificant. Depending on the test format and size, this can be done by adding several points to well-revised essay-type answers, adding a point (or part of a point) for correct multiple choice or fill-in-the-blank-type answers, or by giving full point value for each corrected test item (regardless of the format) and issuing a new test grade that is the average of the initial grade and the recalculated grade.*

Student Created Test

A science teacher is administering a unit test to her sixth-grade class. She directs her students to read over the entire test before beginning. As they do so, one student softly murmurs, "That's my question!"

Another whispers, "Sweet, Joey!"

And a third sighs, "Man, Jarwan, why'd you have to go and write a question about pathogens?"

After a few minutes, the teacher says, "As you can see from the credits at the bottom of your test page, the students in this class produced most of the excellent and challenging questions on this test."

(What It Is:) The *Student Created Test* is a test comprising questions written by students. It helps students think more carefully about material covered during a unit of study.

(Why It's Used:) When studying for a test, students sometimes tend to review material in a perfunctory fashion. By requiring that they formulate viable test questions, the *Student Created Test* compels them to reflect more comprehensively on the subject matter at hand.

(How It's Done:) Assign students to brainstorm and write down possible questions for a test on material covered during their unit of study. (Brainstorming can be done individually, in pairs, or in groups.) Circulate among students to offer encouragement and support where needed. Have your students present some of their questions to the entire class and discuss possible answers, then collect student-created questions and use those that are appropriate when writing the unit test. Cite the student test question authors directly on the test (either beside the question or in footnotes at the bottom of the test). Giving written credit to the test-question authors is a highly beneficial practice that models appropriate citation procedures for your students and provides feelings of confidence and pride to those students whose work is cited.

Perils and Pitfalls: Students sometimes write questions that are too difficult or too easy. Prevent the former by requiring the question writers to know the correct answer to the question they have written and the latter by outlawing questions that require only yes or no, or true or false answers. With less capable students it's a good idea to preclude question-writing confusion by teaching several lessons on formulating useful questions and pairing two students (a strong question formulator with a weak question formulator) to work as a question-writing team.

Variations on a Theme:

- For extra credit use a Jeopardy-type, answer-and-question format, where answers are given and students must supply the questions that produced those answers.

Have the Last Word When Reading

Ten students are working with their teacher in a reading group at two large round tables near the back of their classroom. One is reading aloud and the rest are diligently following along in their books when suddenly the teacher says, "Stop there, Cierra! Everyone please point to the last word Cierra read."

The teacher moves quickly from student to student checking to see if each is pointing to the correct word and then says, "Good job, everyone. I couldn't catch anyone who wasn't with us. Okay, Cierra, continue reading please."

The student reads several more sentences and again the teacher suddenly stops her and directs the students to point to the last word read. "You can't catch me," one boy smilingly teases as the teacher checks to see if he is pointing to the correct word.

"I know, Corey, I can't seem to catch anyone in this group today. Everyone is paying such close attention that we might just finish our reading lesson early today and have a little extra recess time."

(What It Is:) *Have The Last Word When Reading* is a focusing technique. It encourages students to follow along carefully when another student is reading aloud.

(Why It's Used:) In order to strengthen word recognition, word attack, and reading comprehension skills, teachers often direct their students to follow along as another student reads important material aloud. Students who most need to improve their reading skills, however, are often less than attentive during these oral-reading sessions. *Have the Last Word When Reading* helps motivate these students to pay closer attention at such times.

(How It's Done:) At the beginning of an oral-reading session, explain to your students that you are going to stop the person who is reading to see if you can catch someone not following along. Choose

Positive Reinforcement Suggestions

Depending on the age, sophistication level, and sensitivity of your students, positive reinforcement might consist of:

- *Lavish praise and encouragement, "It's wonderful that so many people could follow along and point to the last word read. What a great job! Let's see if we can do even better with the next word we have to point to."*

- *Playful, good-natured teasing-type verbal challenges "Rats! I didn't catch anyone this time. Well, I'm just going to have to try harder to catch some poor unsuspecting soul the next time."*

- *Small food rewards such as a few M&Ms or Goldfish crackers.*

- *Decorative stamps or stickers.*

- *An agreement with the class that for each time everyone accurately points to the last word read the entire class will earn an additional minute of free time or recess.*

a student to read aloudand give several fail-safe demonstrations of the *Have the Last Word When Reading* process.

(**Perils and Pitfalls:**) It can be difficult, if not impossible, to quickly check on every student's tracking when a large number of students are involved. Solve this problem by appointing one or two students as "official checkers."

Also, students who haven't been following along carefully and can't "point to the last word read" may rebel and refuse to participate if their inattention results in negative consequences. You can temper this by presenting *Have the Last Word When Reading* as a game-type challenge and giving lots of positive reinforcement for following along carefully.

(**Variations on a Theme:**)
- Allow the reader to stop and direct the group to point to the last word read or allow the reader to select the next student to read. When using these variations, it's best to set limits on

how many times a student may ask the group to point to the last word read, how much material the reader must cover before calling on another student, and how many times any one student may be selected to read.

- Divide the class into two teams of equally proficient readers and set up a friendly and low-keyed competition to see which team does best at pointing to the last word read.

Hands Down, Ears Open

A social studies teacher is conducting a review lesson on the Revolutionary War. Before beginning, he announces to his class, "Remember, today is a Hands Down, Ears Open *day so I'm not going to wait for you to volunteer. I'm just going to call on people to answer. So be prepared." He then says, "I need someone to tell us about the Boston Tea Party and why it was important to the Revolutionary War."*

He looks around the room and says, " Jovan George, how about you?"

Jovan, a new student who has had little to say during class, responds haltingly with a complete and totally correct answer.

"Great job!" exclaims the surprised teacher. "I think maybe you've been holding back on us, Jovan," he continues, "with answers like that rattling around inside your brain you've got to help us out so we can all learn from you."

"Yeah, man, help us out!" quips the student seated next to Jovan and the class erupts in good-natured laughter.

"Okay, Matthew," responds the teacher with feigned indignation as he focuses on Jovan's talkative neighbor. "Why don't you tell us what a guy named Paul Revere had to do with the Revolutionary War? And don't expect any help from that bright young man seated next to you."

"Aw, man!" sighs Matthew, causing the class to again break into laughter. The class then continues with Matthew answering the question asked him and the teacher calling on students at random. Everyone remains focused and attentive throughout the review knowing that they might be called on to answer at any time.

(**What It Is:**) *Hands Down, Ears Open* is a question-and-answer technique in which teachers do not call on student volunteers to answer questions or participate in discussions, but instead call on them at random.

(**Why It's Used:**) It compels students to pay attention during the lesson and provides more comprehensive class participation. It increases student focus and gives those who might not otherwise participate an opportunity to do so.

(**How It's Done:**) *Hands Down, Ears Open* requires more than simply demanding that students contribute during a lesson. It requires an open and accepting learning environment where students know they will never be ridiculed for offering an incorrect answer. Cultivate this environment early in the school year by establishing from the first day of school that everyone's comments and questions are to be regarded seriously, and that disrespect of others will not be tolerated. In such an environment, *Hands Down, Ears Open* is a useful technique.

Even in the most supportive of environments, however, teachers encounter students who just can't offer an acceptable answer or a student who simply refuses to venture an answer. There are several approaches you can take when this happens:

- Allow every student one refuse-to-answer pass during *Hands Down, Ears Open.*

- Back up and ask the student an easier question. This can be accomplished by making a supportive and empathetic comment such as, "Looks like I started you off with a tough one, Krista. Let's try a warm-up question first," and then ask a question that might require only a yes or no, true or false answer.

- Refuse to draw further attention to the student who does not know an answer and yet tactfully let everyone know the student is still accountable by making a comment such as, "Okay, Charlie, I'll give this one to somebody else, and I'll come back to you with another one before the end of the period."

- Prepare hypersensitive students beforehand by informing them of two or three questions that you might possibly ask them during *Hands Down, Ears Open.*

(**Perils and Pitfalls:**) Use of *Hands Down, Ears Open* in classes lacking supportive, accepting, and respectful learning environments can cause students to rebel or withdraw. They then either refuse to answer, challenge the teacher to make them do so, and/or deliberately offer outlandish answers to disrupt the lesson and deflect attention from themselves. Avoid this ugly scenario by fostering a supportive learning environment before attempting to use *Hands Down, Ears Open.*

If you find yourself faced with a student who refuses to answer you can:

1. Make no comment and simply call on another student.

2. Make a kind and empathetic comment and quickly call on someone else. For example: "Carl really seems puzzled by this one. Mitch, can you help him out?"

3. Tell the silent student you will call on her again later in the lesson and call on another student.

The option you choose depends on your understanding of your students and the dynamics in your classroom at the time. For example, if everyone is cooperative and engaged in the lesson and you call on a student who refuses to answer, the first option is the best choice. However, if the student you call on is sensitive and somewhat shy, the second is probably best. On the other hand, if your students are going through an uncooperative rebellious phase, the third option might be best since it doesn't just let the student refuse to answer but instead puts the class on notice that sooner or later everyone is expected to contribute. If circumstances warrant it, you can then compel your willfully reluctant participant to answer by asking her an extraordinarily simple question.

Variations on a Theme:

- Instead of announcing that the next day's lesson will be a *Hands Down, Ears Open*, simply employ this technique whenever your students appear apprehensive about participating in a lesson. Some middle and high school teachers do not rely on volunteers to contribute to class discussions but instead use this technique exclusively.

- To alleviate students' anxiety, allow them a certain number of free passes (instances when they can pass up answering) during the lesson. Give the student who offers an exceptional answer an extra free pass as a reward.

Cultivating a Supportive Learning Environment

Students feel free to take risks and learn from each other in an environment where everyone is treated with dignity and respect and no one fears ridicule. Such supportive learning environments don't just magically materialize; teachers must take definite measures to build and nurture them. The following are some steps you can take to cultivate a supportive learning environment.

1. Model supportive behavior for your students.

- *Listen carefully when your students are speaking.*

- *Avoid using sarcasm and comedic put-downs. Comments such as: "Come on, Cedric, don't tell me that's your best answer! Your baby brother could do a better job. Use that big head of yours for something other than a hat rack!," may offer some temporary comic relief, but will undermine your students' willingness to take risks and venture answers far into the future.*

- *Be patient and allow your students sufficient time to articulate their thoughts.*

2. Patiently and consistently demand respectful behavior from your students.

- *Insist that your students listen and not talk among themselves when you are teaching or when their classmates are offering answers or asking questions.*

- *Ban disparaging remarks using such words as dummy, stupid, retard, moron, and so forth from your classroom.*

3. Stress that mistakes are an important and necessary part of learning.

- *Freely admit your mistakes, and when possible, allow your students to help you correct them. (For example, if you have just misspelled a word on the board, you might say, "Oops, I think I misspelled the word constitution. Can somebody with a great spelling mind or a dictionary help me out?"*

- *Never criticize students for making mistakes, but instead, emphasize that mistakes are opportunities to learn.*

Build a Break

A teacher is presenting a lesson on parallel sentence construction to her eighth-grade English class, but the students are uncooperative and uninterested. English class is scheduled the last period every day and the teacher must find a way to elicit their cooperation and keep their attention so they can learn the required curriculum.

"Who can tell us if example three is correct?" she asks, looking about the room for volunteers as she does so. Seeing none, she says, "How about you, Desmond? What do you think?"

"I think it's okay," answers Desmond.

"Why do you say that? How do you know it's okay?" probes the teacher.

"'Cause this sentence ends with two nouns with the word 'and' joining them and the sentence that wasn't parallel ended with an adjective and a noun joined by the word 'and'," explains Desmond.

"That's excellent, Desmond!" says the teacher. "I think we can start to build a break with this one." She draws nine blanks on the board, places the letter B above the first one, and asks, "Who wants to tackle example number four?"

This time several students volunteer to answer, the selected student answers correctly, and the teacher writes the letter R in the second blank on the board. The lesson continues with the class motivated and focused on the goal of answering enough questions correctly to spell out the words BREAK TIME on the board. They know that once they achieve that goal the lesson will end and they will have some extra time to chat with their classmates or work on other assignments.

(**What It Is:**) *Build a Break* is a motivational technique. It encourages students to focus and pay attention.

Why It's Used: In order to master difficult concepts, students must focus and attend while those concepts are being taught. Unfortunately, however, in spite of a teacher's best efforts to demonstrate the merits of mastering such concepts, many students are passive and inattentive. *Build a Break* encourages them to actively participate in the lesson by giving them immediate visible reinforcement and a reward for doing so.

How It's Done: *Build a Break* usually works best when it is introduced with an element of surprise and a minimum of explanation. As soon as a student answers a question or makes a significant comment, draw blanks on the board to correspond with the words BREAK TIME (or other words of your choosing) and fill in one blank with a letter. Then, as students become curious and inquire about what your cryptic board blanks might mean, simply continue with the lesson and allow the lesson's conclusion to answer their inquiries. After *Build a Break's* initial use, your students will be aware of this procedure and, in most cases, respond favorably to its use.

Perils and Pitfalls: On rare occasions a few students may remain passive and refuse to participate in the lesson. Depending on their attitude and influence on the other students, you can exclude them from the break time or allow them to participate. One way to deal with this quandary is to allow the students who earned the break time to decide. Another tack you might take is to have the nonparticipants sit quietly for a few minutes and then allow them to join in.

Variations on a Theme:
- In lieu of using the same reward word(s) each time you use this technique, use a mystery word. Draw the number of blanks on the board to correspond with the number of letters in the mystery word, fill in one or two letters as clues, and have your students determine the mystery reward word as the lesson progresses. For example, you might choose a vocabulary term such as PARALLEL CONSTRUCTION, draw twenty

blanks on the board, place two or three letters from the term in the proper blanks, and have your students work toward filling in the rest.

- In addition to vocabulary terms, use words related to pending holidays or students' names as mystery reward words.

Signs That Your Students Are Tuning You Out

Occasionally teachers can get so wrapped up in teaching a lesson that they fail to notice that their quieter, less-assertive students are tuning them out. Although these students aren't disruptive or demanding, they do exhibit behaviors that indicate they are losing interest in the lesson. Among these behaviors are:

- *Failing to make eye contact with the teacher for an extended period of time.*
- *Positioning themselves so they are turned away from the teacher.*
- *Doodling extensively in their notebooks.*
- *Resting their heads in their hands or putting their heads down on their desks.*
- *Staring out of the window or door.*
- *Focusing on the wrong page in the textbook.*
- *Carrying on extensive whispered conversations with their neighbors.*
- *Fiddling with their pens or pencils.*
- *Distracting others by casually bumping their desks or chairs.*

If your students exhibit several of these behaviors during a lesson, you may want to implement some new strategies to liven things up and refocus their attention. Remember, if your quieter, less assertive students are tuning you out, your more assertive students won't be far behind.

Playing Card Pick

A teacher is beginning a lesson and wants to ensure that students are chosen at random to answer questions and participate in a variety of activities. His students react with cheers when he takes two decks of playing cards from his desk and begins shuffling one. He moves around the room dealing two cards to each of the twenty-five students. He then shuffles the deck of cards on his desk, places them aside, and begins teaching the lesson. A few minutes into the lesson he asks a question, chooses a card from the deck on his desk, holds it up for everyone to see, and says, "King of Hearts. Who has the King of Hearts?"

A girl seated in the middle of the room raises her hand timidly.

"Okay, Sherisse. What do you think? Who wrote Stopping by Woods on a Snowy Evening?*"*

"I think it's Walt Whitman," Sherisse replies.

The teacher quickly shuffles the deck of cards on his desk, selects another card, holds it up, and says, "Four of Clubs, do you agree with Sherisse?"

"No, I don't," comes a voice from the back of the room. "I think Robert Frost wrote that poem."

"Good for you, Dominique, a.k.a. the Four of Clubs, you're absolutely correct!" replies the teacher. The lesson then continues with him using the playing cards as a random student-selection tool.

(What It Is:) *Playing Card Pick* is a random selection process. It adds an element of fun to a lesson and objectively affords everyone an opportunity to participate.

(Why It's Used:) *Playing Card Pick* increases student interest and participation during a lesson.

(How It's Done:) Obtain two decks of playing cards. Explain to your students that you are going to deal one deck to them, ask a question, and select a card from the other deck. The student holding a card that is the same as the card you selected must answer the question.

(Perils and Pitfalls:) Since there are fifty-two cards in a standard deck of playing cards and most classes average between twenty to thirty students, there is the possibility you will draw several cards in succession that fail to match those held by students. This can slow down the pace of the lesson and cause students to lose interest. Prevent this by paring down each deck of cards to equal the number of students in your class and double-checking to make sure that the cards retained in one deck are identical to the cards retained in the other.

Also, some students may have religious beliefs that forbid the use of playing cards. If a student in your class has such beliefs, you can excuse that student from participating in this lesson or, should the student seem uncomfortable being excused, create your own random choice cards by writing large numbers on two sets of plain white index cards and dealing those whenever you want to use *Playing Card Pick*.

(Variations on a Theme:)

- Divide the class into several teams, give point values to the cards and their subsequent questions and answers, keep score, and declare the team with the highest score the winner.

- Select several students to be the official dealers for a predetermined number of deals during *Playing Card Pick*.

- Shuffle and deal the cards with great fanfare and add a card trick or two as you do so.

Beach Party

Picture This: *It is nearing the conclusion of an introductory geometry lesson and a quick review of the material covered during the class is needed. The students are a bit fatigued from information overload and anxious for the class to end. The teacher goes to a closet and takes out a beach ball, causing several students to become more attentive. Some smile and applaud silently while others shift in their seats and sit up a little straighter.*

"Okay guys, let's have a Beach Party," the teacher says. "How many degrees in a right angle?" He asks as he tosses the ball toward the back of the room.

An alert student catches it and answers, "A right angle has 90 degrees."

"Right you are, Sophia!" exclaims the teacher.

Sophia smiles and tosses the beach ball back to the teacher who tosses it back to the class as he asks the next question.

What It Is: *Beach Party* is a motivational review technique. It stimulates students to pay attention during the review process.

Why It's Used: *Beach Party* adds pizzazz, fun, and interest to what might otherwise be mundane end-of-lesson reviews.

How It's Done: Buy an inexpensive beach ball. Develop guidelines for using *Beach Party* and review them with your students (see example of guidelines). Employ the *Beach Party* when needed.

Perils and Pitfalls: Overly enthusiastic or blatantly aggressive students can easily wreak havoc during an activity that sanctions throwing objects around the classroom. It is imperative that your students clearly understand the guidelines for participation in *Beach Party*, that those guidelines are enforced, that you participate in this activity modeling appropriate behavior for your students, and that you monitor their behavior throughout.

Example of Beach Party *Guidelines*

1. *The beach ball is to be tossed gently from the teacher to the student and from the student back to the teacher.*

2. *Students who hurl the beach ball fastball style will be disqualified from participation.*

3. *The student who catches the ball is responsible for answering the question.*

4. *If the student who catches the ball cannot answer the question, he or she may toss the ball gently to another student to answer the question.*

5. *If three different students have the ball tossed gently to them and cannot answer the question, the ball must be tossed back to the teacher.*

6. *The teacher will stop* Beach Party *if students frequently fail to follow the guidelines.*

Variations on a Theme:

- Vary the questioning order. Toss the ball first and after it is caught, ask a question. Ask a question first and then toss the ball.

- Have the student who catches the ball ask a question and toss the ball to a classmate to answer it.

- If the beach ball is multicolored, use the colors to determine who will or will not answer a question. For example, immediately after the ball is caught you might say, "Blue is the bonus color. If one of your hands is on blue, you get to toss the ball to someone else without answering the question."

Basketball Free Throw Review

A class is excitedly reviewing material for a future test. At the front of the room is a small Nerf-type basketball hoop. On the floor a few feet away, horizontal to the bottom of the hoop holder, is a long strip of masking tape.

"All right everyone, listen up," commands the teacher. "The next question is a three pointer."

The students nudge one another and giggle nervously. "If it's a three pointer, it's gonna be a toughie," whispers one student to another.

"What are two ways historians hypothesize that early man got to the Americas thousands of years before the first European explorers?" asks the teacher.

A small girl seated near the front of the room raises her hand tentatively.

"Ah, yes, Tyesha. You want to take a try at this challenging three pointer?" remarks the teacher.

"Okay! Okay! I know this one. Just let me think for a minute," says Tyesha, smiling shyly. "Historians hypothesize that some early men and WOMEN," she begins, stressing the word, "walked across a land bridge between Asia and North America and other early men and WOMEN came across the Pacific Ocean on crudely made rafts."

"Very good, Tyesha! You are exactly right! That answer earns you the right to move to the free throw line and shoot three."

(What It Is:) *Basketball Free Throw Review* is a motivational review strategy. It keeps students actively involved in the review process.

(Why It's Used:) Review lessons are essential to subject matter mastery, yet students often participate half-heartedly in the usual paper-and-pencil or oral question-and-answer type review. The *Basketball Free Throw Review* stimulates interest and enthusiasm, especially among sports-minded students.

(How It's Done:) Purchase a Nerf-type basketball hoop, stand, and basketball from your local discount toy store (these can sometimes be purchased for a couple of dollars at yard sales or obtained as a donation from parents whose kids have outgrown the toy). Formulate review questions and set point values for them. While a score in basketball is worth either one, two, or three points, you may wish to give more difficult questions an even higher point value. If you choose to do this, however, be prepared for complaints from your basketball purists. Place the basketball hoop against a wall in an easily accessible area of the classroom. Mark a free throw line on the floor a few feet in front of the hoop using a strip of masking tape or a piece of cord taped to the floor, taking care not to damage the flooring. Since the purpose of this activity is to keep your students focused and attentive, not frustrated and angry, initially put the free throw line where the majority of your students can easily make a basket. Develop a few basic common-sense rules for using *Basketball Free Throw Review* specific to your class (see examples that follow). Review these with your students. Use *Basketball Free Throw Review* as warranted.

(Perils and Pitfalls:) At times during *Basketball Free Throw Reviews* classroom noise can reach unacceptable levels. This is especially true when students are cheering for and celebrating a classmate's accomplishments. Control high noise levels by suspending the review and reminding students that it cannot continue if it disrupts nearby classes.

Also, use of *Basketball Free Throw Review* can be the bane of athletically disinclined students who dread the prospect of shooting free throws in front of the entire class. Protect these students from ridicule (real or imagined) and ease their anxiety by allowing any student who answers a question correctly to select a substitute to shoot his or her free throw(s). This not only allows the athletically disinclined student to save face, but also gives him or her enormous power and status among his or her classmates.

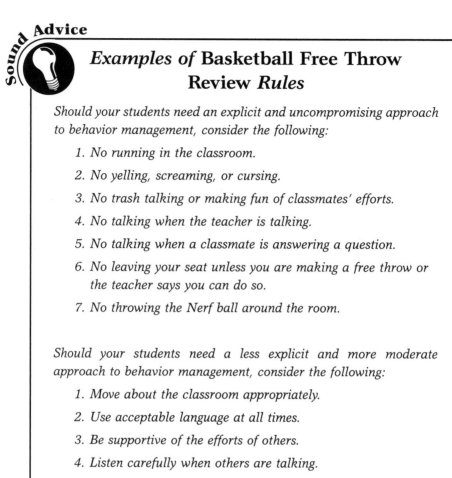

Examples of Basketball Free Throw Review *Rules*

Should your students need an explicit and uncompromising approach to behavior management, consider the following:

1. *No running in the classroom.*

2. *No yelling, screaming, or cursing.*

3. *No trash talking or making fun of classmates' efforts.*

4. *No talking when the teacher is talking.*

5. *No talking when a classmate is answering a question.*

6. *No leaving your seat unless you are making a free throw or the teacher says you can do so.*

7. *No throwing the Nerf ball around the room.*

Should your students need a less explicit and more moderate approach to behavior management, consider the following:

1. *Move about the classroom appropriately.*

2. *Use acceptable language at all times.*

3. *Be supportive of the efforts of others.*

4. *Listen carefully when others are talking.*

5. *Remain seated unless you are making a free throw.*

6. *Use the Nerf to make free throws only.*

Variations on a Theme:

- Set up a spirited competition by dividing the class into two teams and keeping score. Be sure the teams are fairly balanced with equal numbers of athletically inclined and/or academically inclined students on both teams.

- If the gymnasium is available and with permission of the physical education department, take the class to the gym for this activity and allow students who answer questions correctly to make stupendous dunk shots and show off their hoops prowess for their classmates.

- Discuss with the physical education teacher the possibility of combining a portion of a physical education lesson on basketball with an academic review lesson.

Who Wants to Be a Millionaire?

A class is beginning the question-and-answer review part of a lesson. The teacher removes a stack of play money from her desk and says, "Let's use Who Wants to Be a Millionaire? *for our review."*

Immediately several hands shoot into the air. "Can I be the banker?" asks the first child called on by the teacher.

"I'm afraid not, Tim. Remember the last time we played a class game I promised Marvin he'd have a special job, so he gets to be the banker," responds the teacher as she hands the stack of play money to a tall, thin boy seated near the classroom door.

She continues. "The class's target goal for today's review is $200. As soon as the amount of money earned by the students in this class totals $200, the review will end and you all can have some free time. Also, keep in mind that so far this year the top individual money winners to beat are Rosco, who has earned $175, and Susan, who has earned $160."

"Now everyone listen carefully," the teacher continues. "The first question is worth $10." She takes a sheet of questions from her desk, scans it quickly, and asks, "What are two major elements that comprise air?"

A child seated in the middle of the room whispers quietly, "I know! I know!" as he raises his hand.

"Okay, Amir. You think you can handle this one? Let's hear it," says the teacher as she calls on Amir.

"Two major elements in air are oxygen and nitrogen," answers Amir.

"Right you are, Amir! Banker, give that man his $10!" exclaims the teacher playfully. "All right gang, a correct answer to the next question is worth $20. Pay close attention now, 'cause this one is a toughie."

(**What It Is:**) Who Wants to Be a Millionaire? is a motivational review strategy. It provides immediate tangible reinforcement to attentive and knowledgeable students.

Why It's Used: It encourages student participation in review lessons and reinforces money-calculation skills through the use of an enjoyable, understandable, and unusual format.

How It's Done: Obtain a supply of play money. Review the *Who Wants to Be a Millionaire?* procedure with your students (see example below). Use *Who Wants to Be a Millionaire?* when feasible.

Sound Advice

Examples of Who Wants to be a Millionaire? *Procedures*

1. *Before the game begins, the teacher will select a student to be the official banker and announce the total amount of money the class must earn in order to gain free time.*

2. *The teacher will read the question, announce the money value of the correct answer, and determine if an answer is correct.*

3. *When a student gives a correct answer, the official banker will pay him or her, record the amount of money each student earns, and keep a record of the total amount earned by the class.*

4. *Once the class earns its goal amount, the review will end and the class will have free time.*

5. *Free time will continue until the end of the period, subject to appropriate student behavior.*

Perils and Pitfalls: When students earn their goal amount during a *Who Wants to be a Millionaire?* review lesson too quickly, the result can lead to disciplinary problems caused by too much unstructured time. The solution, of course, is to set the goal amount high enough so that students can attain it with only a short time left in the period.

- Write the questions with their dollar values on slips of paper, fold the slips, place them in a hat, and have students draw one at random each time a new question is needed.

- Divide the class into teams and have a competition to see which team collects the most money.

Part II

Let's Do It All Together

Strategies That Encourage Cooperation and Teamwork

 **Part II**

- Teaming for Research
- Silent Scavenger Hunt
- Group Research Race
- Hallway Orienteering
- Relay Race Review
- Great Mountaineering Race

The Joy of Teaching a Cohesive
and Cooperative Class

As a second-year teacher, I learned a valuable lesson about the joy and importance of teaching students to work together cooperatively. After a difficult and marginally successful first year, I was determined to improve during my second and resolutely set about to do so. I formulated student guidelines, explained and enforced them with consistency, and carefully planned lessons appropriate for my students' grade and ability levels.

Things began so well that the principal of the middle school where I taught, a grizzled veteran of many past teaching campaigns, actually complimented me for getting off to such a good start. This was indeed encouraging, since based on my first year's chaotic classes, I was currently assigned the classroom directly across the hall from the office so, if need be, my principal could more readily step in and restore order.

With this positive feedback from my principal and observable evidence that my students were learning, my teaching confidence grew. I started planning lessons that allowed them more freedom and encouraged them to work together in groups. I insisted, however, that they follow specific procedures for group work and held them accountable for the output of their groups, and they responded well to the structured freedom afforded them. When assigned a group project, they accepted their assignments, and team members, with a minimum of complaint, selected group leaders and note takers, discussed their projects, and set about to complete them. I, of course, was just bursting with pride and newly found teaching acumen, but the best was yet to come.

On a cold and rainy morning in early November, my car battery died, and after calling AAA, I contacted my principal to let him know that I'd be arriving late. My first-period class was scheduled to work on finalizing their group research papers, but because I wasn't going to be there, I told my principal to direct my substitute to use my emergency plans. When I finally arrived at school at the very end of the first period and rushed into my classroom, I expected to find a substitute teacher and peevish students. Instead, I found my students seated in groups working away on their research reports and no teacher to be found. At that moment my principal stuck his head in the door and motioned me into the hall; my heart sank.

He said, "I just wanted to let you know that you've done an outstanding job with this class. I couldn't find coverage for you this morning so I covered your class myself. I was going to use your emergency plans as you directed, but your students told me they were working on some interesting projects and knew exactly what they were supposed to do. They politely informed me that they could take care of themselves, and didn't need a babysitter. I figured I'd give them enough rope to hang themselves and went across the hall to my office and watched what was happening from there. I have to admit your guys stayed focused on the job at hand and did a good job. When the noise level in the class got too high, they reminded one another to keep it down and when there was a problem in a group, the group worked together to solve it. It was amazing. I wish all of my teachers could get their students to work so well together. It would sure make my job a lot easier."

A Word About *Let's Do It All Together*

Your students' ability to cooperate and collaborate effectively is essential, not only to daily classroom harmony but also to their future success. Classrooms in which students support one another and work together well are positive places where learning easily takes place. Employers value employees who listen respectfully and attentively to the contributions of others and are comfortable working with them to solve problems.

Developing teamwork skills in immature and self-centered youngsters is a challenge that requires planning, patience, and perseverance, as well as some creative, methodological derring-do. Each activity in this section encourages students to work collaboratively and cooperatively to achieve a common goal, compels them to actively participate in working toward its achievement, and keeps them constructively engaged throughout the entire process.

Teaming for Research

A teacher is speaking to his fourth-period history class. "You all know that as part of our new unit on the history of the American West you must complete a research project on a Native American tribe."

(The class makes a slightly audible groan.)

"This project, however, is different because it is a team research project," continues the teacher.

"What's a team research project?" asks a student seated near the back of the room.

"A team research project is just what its name implies," answers the teacher. "It is research that a group of students works on together as a team with each member of the group responsible for one part of the research."

"What do you mean, 'responsible for one part of the research?'" asks another student skeptically.

"Well, for example, a group will be assigned to find out information about the Apaches. So one person in the group might research the history of the Apaches in the West, another might research the food, clothing, and shelter used by the Apaches, and another might find out about the treaties the Apaches made with the U.S. government and the nearby settlers," explains the teacher.

(What It Is:) *Teaming for Research* is a collaborative research method. It affords students the opportunity to work together to complete a research report and present their information in novel or creative ways.

(Why It's Used:) *Teaming for Research* helps students acquire a great deal of information on an assigned topic quickly, develop requisite skills for working with others, and improve their individual research skills.

How It's Done: Choose research topics appropriate for your class. Make sure the selected topics contain several researchable subtopics (for example, a specific historical period, a noted author's literary works, or a famous inventor's inventions). Develop specific guidelines for the team research project and review them with your students (see sample guidelines).

Sound Advice

Sample Team Research Guidelines

1. Research topics and work groups are assigned by the teacher and not open to discussion or debate.

2. Every team member must research and hand in a written report on one major subtopic of his group's main topic.

3. Every team member must share the information in his written report with the other members of his team.

4. All team members are responsible for all of the research information shared with them on each subtopic.

5. Each team is responsible for sharing with the class the information they have learned about their assigned topic.

6. Students will receive an individual grade for their independent subtopic research report, a grade for their overall knowledge of the entire topic, and a team grade for the total topic presentation that is made to the class.

7. Students who cannot work cooperatively will be removed from their team and will be required to complete the entire project independently. Those remaining on the team will not be accountable for the research of any team members removed for wasting research time.

Perils and Pitfalls: Students sometimes object to working with the other students assigned to their group or lobby to work with a group comprising only their friends. Prevent such objections and lobbying efforts by developing and patiently enforcing guidelines you establish at the outset.

Also, class periods allocated for research can deteriorate into student socialization sessions, and problems can occur when one member of a group does not satisfactorily complete his part of the research report. Limit the incidence of nonproductive work sessions and less-than-stellar performance from individual team members by:

- Insisting everyone adhere to very specific research guidelines as well as a task-timeline checklist (see example of timeline checklist below).

- Visiting with the various research groups as they work.

- Closely monitoring each group's research plan as well as their progress toward completing it.

- Having each team fill in a task completion checklist for each day's work (see sample checklist).

- Providing suggestions, guidance, and motivation as necessary.

Variations on a Theme:

- Make a comprehensive book on the main topic (for example, Famous Native American Tribes of the Southwest United States) by combining the written reports from each team.

- Have the teams select their research topics from a list of topics.

- Allow students to select the team members with whom they wish to work. (When using this variation, be prepared to deal with the problem of the nonselected student.)

- Randomly choose team members by drawing names from a hat.

Example of a Teaming for Research *Task-Timeline Checklist*

Objective: To complete a group research report and presentation on a selected topic with each group member contributing a significant portion of written research to the overall report.

Time Allotment: Seven class periods over a 3–4 week time span with students responsible for any additional time needed to complete research and prepare their group reports and presentations. *(Time allotments must be adjusted to address the research skills and work habits of students.)*

Team Research Project • Day One

Meet with team members. . . . . ❏

Elect team leader and note taker. . . . . ❏

Divide report into subtopics. . . . . ❏

Each team member selects a subtopic. . . . . ❏

Recorder records researchers' names and their subtopic
responsibilities and gives the list to the teacher . . . . ❏

Team Research Project • Day Two
(Class to be held in the Media/Technology Center)

Meet with team members. . . . . ❏

Review the project's subtopic assignments. . . . . ❏

Each team member:

   Locates at least two useful sources. . . . . ❏

   Records at least six facts. . . . . ❏

Team leader checks progress made by team members. . . . . ❏

Recorder fills in timeline checklist and
gives it to the teacher. . . . . ❏

(continued on next page)

Team Research Project • Day Three
(Class to be held in the Media/Technology Center)

Meet with team members.......................... ❑

Review the progress each team member has made
on his or her subtopic research...................... ❑

Each team member:

    Locates at least two useful sources.................. ❑

    Records at least six facts........................ ❑

Team leader checks progress made by team members........ ❑

Recorder fills in timeline checklist and
gives it to the teacher............................ ❑

Team Research Project • Day Four
(Class to be held in the Media/Technology Center)

Meet with team members.......................... ❑

Review the progress each team member has
made on his or her subtopic research. .... ❑

All team members continue to locate and
record facts from sources.......................... ❑

All team members begin writing their
subtopic report. .... ❑

Team leader checks progress made by
team members................................. ❑

Recorder fills in timeline checklist and
gives it to the teacher............................ ❑

*(Team members to complete written reports independently
before next team meeting.)*

(continued on next page)

Team Research Project • Day Five

Meet with team members. . . . . ❏

Each team member distributes a copy of his or
her subtopic report to everyone on the team and
reviews the report with the team. ❏

Team leader moderates any discussion about
the individual reports. . . . . ❏

Team begins work on combining subtopic reports
into one report. . . . . ❏

Recorder fills in timeline checklist and
gives it to the teacher. . . . . ❏

Team Research Project • Day Six

Meet with team members. . . . . ❏

Team continues and completes work on
combining subtopic reports into one report
and prepares class presentation. ❏

Recorder fills in timeline checklist and
gives it to the teacher. . . . . ❏

Team Research Project • Day Seven

Team shares report information with the class. . . . . ❏

Each team member gives a copy of his or her
subtopic report to the teacher. . . . . ❏

A copy of the team report is given to the teacher. . . . . ❏

Recorder gives the completed timeline
checklist to the teacher. . . . . ❏

Silent Scavenger Hunt

It is a cold rainy November afternoon. A teacher is alone in her classroom grading papers when three students knock at the door. She looks up, smiles, and signals to them to come in. They enter silently and one of them hands her a note that reads: "Mr. Edwards' class is having a silent scavenger hunt. We have a list of objects we must collect, take back to Mr. Edwards' room, and then return to the exact place where we found them. Since the hunt is held in total silence, we cannot talk and must use other means of communicating with you."

The students point to their scavenger list and to a small world globe at the back of the room. The teacher smiles and says, "Okay, guys, you can borrow my globe, on the condition that you bring it back and place it exactly where you found it."

The students nod their heads in agreement, take the globe, and hurry off to Mr. Edwards' room, giggling softly as they do so.

(What It Is:) *Silent Scavenger Hunt* is an enjoyable team activity that permits students to move about the school in a relaxed, yet nondisruptive manner. It encourages cooperation and develops practical problem-solving skills, and is most useful in assuaging student disappointment when inclement weather or an emergency forces the cancellation or postponement of a highly anticipated special activity such as sports day or a field trip.

(Why It's Used:) Before using this activity, inform neighboring teachers that your class will hold a *Silent Scavenger Hunt* and give each teacher a copy of the game's guidelines.

Explain the guidelines and rules carefully to your students. Stress that they must respect the rights of teachers who choose not to participate or permit scavengers access to their classrooms, must return all "scavenged" materials to their original locations, and must take great care not to disturb other classes.

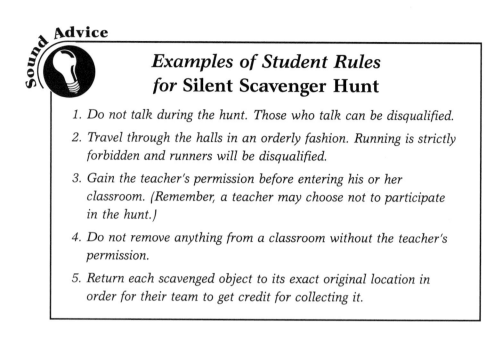

Examples of Student Rules
for Silent Scavenger Hunt

1. *Do not talk during the hunt. Those who talk can be disqualified.*

2. *Travel through the halls in an orderly fashion. Running is strictly forbidden and runners will be disqualified.*

3. *Gain the teacher's permission before entering his or her classroom. (Remember, a teacher may choose not to participate in the hunt.)*

4. *Do not remove anything from a classroom without the teacher's permission.*

5. *Return each scavenged object to its exact original location in order for their team to get credit for collecting it.*

(**Perils and Pitfalls:**) Regardless of guidelines and warnings, overly exuberant *Silent Scavenger Hunt* participants do, at times, create problems by "walking" through the halls at breakneck speed. This can be addressed by establishing a "time out" penalty for speedy scavengers. Also, students are sometimes careless about returning scavenged items to their original locations. Solve this problem by asking teachers from whom items are borrowed to initial the scavenger's "hunt list" next to the name of their loaned item when it is returned appropriately.

The best way to prevent overall *Silent Scavenger* behavior problems is to avoid placing several troublesome students on the same team and to appoint a few student judges to help assure that the hunt's rules are followed. However, a *Silent Scavenger Hunt* is a highly motivational and engaging activity that offers students a positive learning experience and seldom causes serious behavior problems.

Example of a Letter Informing
Staff Members of Silent Scavenger Hunt

Dear Staff Member,

Tomorrow, as a special activity, my third-period class will participate in a Silent Scavenger Hunt. *The hunt requires teams of students to collect various items from around the school, bring them to my classroom for verification, and return the items to their exact original location. Participants may not talk during the hunt and are strictly forbidden from entering any classroom or removing any item from a classroom without the teacher's permission. The scavenger teams must, of course, ask for permission without speaking.*

If for any reason you wish not to participate, please let me know as soon as possible or simply inform my students you are not participating should they arrive at your classroom.

> *Sincerely,*
>
> *Ms. Scavenger*

Variations on a Theme:

- Instead of giving student teams duplicate lists of all the objects to be found during the hunt, have each team draw a slip of paper with the name of the next object to be found only after they have found the previous object.

- In lieu of a specific object such as a world globe, have students hunt for an object with a general characteristic such as a multicolored sphere.

Group Research Race

Groups of students are working on research in a school's library or technology center. Each group has a different set of research questions. Some students move quickly and purposefully about looking for books and periodicals that contain the answers to the questions on their list, while others conduct computer-based searches for those answers. A student finds the answer to a question, returns to his group's table, and writes the answer on the group's answer sheet.

"I found it! The dude's name is Oliver Wendell Holmes," comments one boy as he records his answer.

"Nice, B.J.!" exclaims a boy who is busily searching through an almanac at the table. "Just three more answers and our group will be finished. I think maybe we're gonna set a new Research Race record!"

(**What It Is:**) *Group Research Race* is a highly focused, fast-paced activity that challenges student work groups to complete a short-term research project as quickly as possible. It prompts students to perform research and helps them develop skills locating answers to factual questions quickly and efficiently.

(**Why It's Used:**) Students are often apathetic about completing research assignments because they view them as overwhelming and boring. *Group Research Race* helps diminish such research apathy by showing students the many resources readily available to help them accomplish research and adding the elements of peer support and competitive fun.

(**How It's Done:**) Prepare a set of short-answer, fact-based questions that can be answered using the research resources readily available in your school. (To insure your students' success, it's best to ascertain that the answers can actually be found using your school's research resources.) Introduce the *Group Research Race* concept to your students and review the guidelines for the race. Divide the class into work groups and distribute a set of research questions to each group. Allow students sufficient time to complete the assignment, while providing encouragement and oversight as necessary. Record unofficial times as the groups complete their research. (Inform students that times become official only after a group's answers have been more thoroughly checked.)

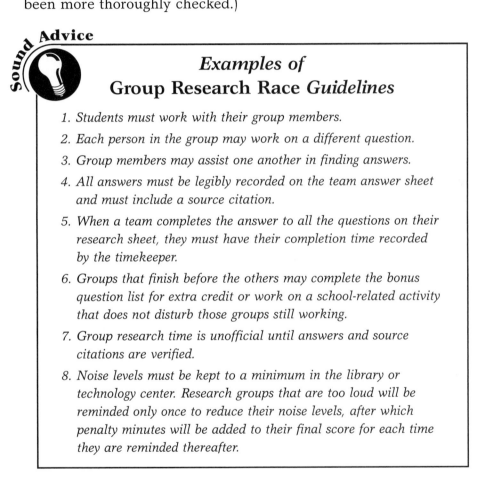

Sound Advice

Examples of
Group Research Race *Guidelines*

1. *Students must work with their group members.*
2. *Each person in the group may work on a different question.*
3. *Group members may assist one another in finding answers.*
4. *All answers must be legibly recorded on the team answer sheet and must include a source citation.*
5. *When a team completes the answer to all the questions on their research sheet, they must have their completion time recorded by the timekeeper.*
6. *Groups that finish before the others may complete the bonus question list for extra credit or work on a school-related activity that does not disturb those groups still working.*
7. *Group research time is unofficial until answers and source citations are verified.*
8. *Noise levels must be kept to a minimum in the library or technology center. Research groups that are too loud will be reminded only once to reduce their noise levels, after which penalty minutes will be added to their final score for each time they are reminded thereafter.*

(Perils and Pitfalls:) When groups are declared winners while the race is ongoing, the others can lose their motivation to continue working industriously. Stave off such motivational malaise by having groups estimate the time they will need to complete their research before the race begins and encouraging them to work toward meeting or beating their estimates. Be sure, however, to provide guidance to help groups arrive at reasonable and fair time estimates.

Also, in their zeal to win, students may simply write down the first answer they come to without taking the necessary time to verify its correctness. Discourage rushed and haphazard work by setting a minimum research time limit before which no team results will be reviewed and adding penalty minutes to a team's final time score for each incorrect answer.

Handwriting that is barely legible can present another problem. A guideline stating that answers must be written legibly, along with the suggestion that groups might want to ask someone with legible hand-writing (or excellent keyboarding skills) to be their "official answer recorder," usually solves this problem.

Variations on a Theme:

- Have two groups complete the same research questions. (It is not necessary to inform them that they are doing so.) Use a comparison of the answers from the two groups to quickly pinpoint problem research areas.

- Start a competition between several classes by calculating and posting the average research time required by all the groups in each class.

Hallway Orienteering

A group of students is huddled around a floor plan of the school and map of the school grounds.

"Look, it says right here, 'From the west side front school entrance travel east to the first doorway on the south.' Well, the first doorway on the south is the guidance office. So let's go!" directs a student.

The students move down the hall, stop in front of the first doorway on the south, and write the words "guidance office" on their answer sheets.

"Where do we go next?" asks another student.

"It says to head east to the second stairway on the north, descend the stairs and travel west to the fourth classroom on the north," a student reads from the direction sheet.

The group heads east, descends the second stairway on the north, travels west, locates the correct classroom, and marks its number on their answer sheets.

"That makes ten. We can head back to social studies and hand in our sheets or we can do the Extra Credit stuff. Wha' cha think?" asks the student with the direction sheet.

"Dude, this is kinda fun. I'm for doin' the extra stuff," answers a tall, thin boy as the rest of the group murmurs its assent.

(What It Is:) *Hallway Orienteering* is a collaborative study activity. It builds skills in map reading and following directions, while demonstrating to students the value of working together cooperatively.

(Why It's Used:) It gives students "structured freedom," allows them to work together to achieve a common goal, and provides them with a modified orienteering experience.

(How It's Done:) Discuss the proposed orienteering lesson with your school's administration. Prepare an accurate and viable set of orienteering directions and a set of guidelines that coincide with your school's policies and procedures. Be sure to vary each group's directions so that several groups do not congregate in the same area of the school simultaneously. Review the directions and guidelines with your students. Provide each group with a small compass or, in lieu of a compass, review the school's directional orientation with your class. (For example, the main entrance is on the north side of the building, the playing fields are on the west side, and so forth). Begin the project.

(Perils and Pitfalls:) A successful *Hallway Orienteering* project requires much teacher pre-planning and preparation. This extra workload can be greatly reduced by teaming with other teachers to plan and implement this lesson; however, a carefully designed orienteering lesson can be used year after year with revisions to meet the educational needs and the skills levels of current classes.

Excited students can easily become disorderly while orienteering and teams sometimes get totally off track and have no idea they have done so. Address these potential problems by having orienteering judges (adult hall monitors) present and requiring each team to check with a judge after every two or three "identified" destinations. These check-ins have a settling effect on excited students and should a judge discover a team has identified the wrong destinations and is hopelessly off course, he or she can direct students back to a correct location and have them progress from there.

(Variations on a Theme:)

- Have student groups plan orienteering exercises and exchange them with other student groups for orienteering.

- Plan the orienteering project for use outside on school grounds.

Relay Race Review

The students in a class are standing at the back of their classroom in five groups. Each group of students is in a line, one behind another. The desks in the room are arranged so that there are five clear pathways leading to the front chalkboard and that chalkboard is divided into five distinct columns.

"Are all teams ready to begin?" the teacher inquires with feigned importance.

The students respond with a resounding, "Yes," and the teacher reaches into a paper bag, pulls out a slip of paper, and says, "The word is 'antibiotic'. The doctor prescribed a strong antibiotic to fight the patient's infection. Antibiotic."

As soon as the teacher has finished pronouncing "antibiotic" the final time she says, "All racers on your mark, get ready, get set, go!"

The first student on each team walks quickly down his team's pathway to his corresponding column on the chalkboard, picks up a piece of chalk, and prints the letter "A" on the board. He then walks quickly back to his team and hands the chalk to the next team member. That team member walks quickly to his team's board space and writes the letter "N" next to the letter "A." This process continues until each team completes their spelling of antibiotic at the board.

The teacher says, "Team three was first across the finish line, but before we can declare a winner, we have to see which teams spelled 'antibiotic' correctly." She moves to the front board and checks each letter of each team's spelling of antibiotic. She starts with the team that crossed the finish line last and ends with the team that crossed the finish line first and amid cheers from team three, declares them the official winner of the "antibiotic" race. She then directs the relay teams to get ready for the next word and Relay Race Review continues.

(**What It Is:**) The *Relay Race Review* is an enjoyable, low-stress, high-activity review method. It uses a relay race format to review previously taught material.

(**Why It's Used:**) It helps students focus and actively participate in a review lesson and encourages them to work together as a team.

(**How It's Done:**) Organize your students and arrange the class-room to accommodate the relay format (such as that described in the above scenario). Carefully explain the rules that students must follow to participate in the relay. Provide good-humored structure and support throughout the activity.

Sound Advice

Examples of
Relay Race Review *Guidelines*

1. *Team members must stand in a straight line when waiting to race.*

2. *The first racers must wait until the teacher says, "Go" before crossing the starting line. All other racers must wait until the student racing for their team hands them his piece of chalk before beginning.*

3. *All writing on the chalkboard must be legible.*

4. *Racers may not run. Runners will be disqualified.*

5. *The referee will determine which team finishes first.*

6. *Since this is an indoor activity, the noise level must be kept down. The relay will be temporarily suspended if the noise level becomes too high.*

(**Perils and Pitfalls:**) Excessive student enthusiasm during a *Relay Race Review* can at times escalate into raucous screaming, celebratory high-five dancing, and contestants "walking" toward the finish line at breakneck speeds. Dampen such excessive and inappro-priate enthusiasm by patiently and amiably enforcing the *Relay Race*

Review rules and temporarily suspending the race if behavior becomes intolerable. Also, since *Relay Race Review* is a simplistic game-type activity that does not provide an in-depth review of subject matter, consider employing it only when reviewing basic factual information such as spelling and vocabulary words, historic dates and people, math facts and formulas, and so forth.

Variations on a Theme:

- Allow team members to collaborate on an answer before starting the relay part of the race. For example, ask the question, provide a brief consultation period, and then direct the first racers to take their marks.

- Have students race backwards.

- Choose students to be the race officials such as the starter, question reader, referee, and so forth.

Great Mountaineering Race

A class is actively participating in a review game. The students are divided into two teams. Clipped to the chalkboard at the front of the classroom is a large drawing of a mountain. The mountain is divided into twenty horizontal levels. A cutout picture of a mountain climber is attached to the left hand side of the mountain resting on the fifth level. A second cutout picture of a mountain climber is attached to the right hand side resting on the fourth level.

The teacher reaches into a basket filled with folded slips of paper, pulls one out, and says, "Okay, Team One, this question goes to you. Let's see if you guys can catch up to Team Two." He then reads from the slip, "What is the major function of the body's lymphatic system?"

The students on the left hand side of the room immediately huddle together and begin whispering among themselves. After a minute, the huddle disperses and a student answers, "The main function of the lymphatic system is to fight infection."

"That answer is correct, Team One," says the teacher. "Someone from Team One please go to the mountain and move your mountaineer up the mountain one level," he continues with mock officiousness.

The members of Team One cheer and celebrate with restrained high-fives until the teacher stops them by saying, "Team Two, Team One is hot on your heels. You need this answer to stay ahead of them on the mountain." He pulls another question slip from the basket and reads, "Due to a blizzard, your mountaineering team must stay put for one night. You miss the chance to answer a question and advance up the mountain."

The students on Team One laugh and cheer while the students on Team Two offer words of encouragement to one another.

What It Is: *Great Mountaineering Race* is competitive review activity. It keeps students involved and interested during what otherwise might be a routine review lesson.

Why It's Used: Students' attention frequently wanes during run-of-the-mill review lessons. *Great Mountaineering Race* uses the spirit of competition and a game-type format to liven things up and improve overall attention.

How It's Done: Prior to using *Great Mountaineering Race* with your class, complete a large, chart-paper or tag-board drawing of a mountain and two mountain climbers. (If you are not artistically inclined, accomplish this by using a computer and chart-maker software or by projecting a line drawing overhead transparency of a mountain and two climbers onto chart paper and tracing them.)

Sound Advice

Additional Comments for the Great Mountaineering Race *Question Slips*

- *Lost your footing. Slide down the mountain two levels.*
- *Wind at your back. Move up one level.*
- *Ran out of oxygen. Return to base camp and start over from there.*
- *Found easy passageway. Move up two levels.*
- *Fell in crevasse. Lose a turn.*
- *Foreign guide doesn't understand you. Other team gets to answer question.*
- *Other team lost in snow squall. Your team moves up three levels.*
- *Backpack lost. Lose a turn.*
- *Sunny day. Move up two levels.*
- *Mountain goat shows you new trail up the mountain. Move up two levels.*
- *Rope caught on rock. Go down one level.*

Cut out the mountain and mountaineers. Draw lines across the mountain dividing it into several horizontal sections. (You may want to laminate these materials to increase their durability and save future preparation time.) Prepare a set of question slips. Describe *Great Mountaineering Race* to your students and model for them how it's played. Set guidelines appropriate for the social, emotional, and educational levels of your students.

(Perils and Pitfalls:) The visual props for *Great Mountaineering Race* require extensive preparation time. The time is well spent, however, since the materials prove useful for many years to come.

Student teams participating in *Great Mountaineering Race* sometimes take an inordinate amount of time in the huddle. Avoid this by setting time limits (for example, no more than one minute of discussion per team per question) and appointing a student to be the official time-keeper throughout the game.

(Variations on a Theme:)

- In lieu of teams, have the entire class work together to climb the mountain. When the class reaches the top, the review is complete.

- Have students select and read the "climbing questions."

- Have students write the questions to be used in the mountain climb.

- Add some "fun" comment slips to the question slip basket. These might contain comments such as, "slide down the mountain two levels," "move up one level," or "pass this question to the next team."

Part III

Let's Get It All Together

Strategies That Keep Students Organized

 **Inside Part III**

- Remember John Hancock for Younger Students
- Remember John Hancock for Older Students
- Just Scrap It Writing
- Just Scrap It Practice
- Contents List Procrastination Preventive
- Notebook Model
- Color Coded Work Folders
- Have Question, Will Travel
- Visit from Inspector Clouseau

Lessons Taught by a Dynamo of Disorganization

He was just a little guy with glasses, a cowlick, and a beguiling grin, but boy, did he wreak disorganized havoc on my fourth-grade class! His desk was crammed full of crumpled and torn papers, textbooks, dog-eared workbooks, rumpled work folders, broken pencils, used tissues, and empty cellophane candy wrappers that overflowed onto the floor and caused complaints from neighboring classmates: "Jeffrey's junk is in my area again!"

Changes from one academic subject to another that required a different textbook, workbook, or work folder became exasperating adventures with everyone watching in amazement as Jeffery rummaged haphazardly through the ever-burgeoning contents of his over-taxed desk, and after several minutes of relentless searching, threw caution to the wind and emptied half its contents onto the floor before finally holding up the requested material in triumph, announcing, "Here it is! Here's my reading folder! I finally found it!"

Clearly, Jeffrey's lack of organization was having a deleterious effect on everyone and something had to be done to help him get better organized. After some thought, I decided on a three-pronged attack plan. First, I obtained a large cardboard box, covered it with colored paper, labeled it "Jeffrey's Books," and placed it beside Jeffrey's desk. I stressed to Jeffrey that only books and absolutely nothing else could be put in his book-box, and that he would lose one minute of recess for every object other than a book that I found in his book box whenever I held a surprise book box inspection. Next, so the folders for different subjects could easily be distinguished from one another without the need for rummaging, I had everyone in the class make work folders from large sheets of colored paper and assigned a specific color for each subject. Finally, I appointed Jeffrey "Clean-Up Captain," a job requiring him, after cleaning up his own area, to take the trash can around the room at the end of the day and remind his classmates to clean up their areas.

Needless to say my attack plan didn't work perfectly, Jeffrey's desk still built up clutter throughout the day, his book box had a tendency to stray from his desk, and frequently he would withdraw several broken pencil shards before coming up with a useable nub. But he did develop a rather vague understanding of the concept, "a place for everything and everything in its place," and his lesson-halting rummaging was significantly reduced, as was his teacher's stress level.

A Word About Let's Get It All Together

Poorly organized students can seriously impede their own and everyone else's learning progress. Students who fail to place their names on their papers, keep organized notebooks, or hand in long-term assignments promptly, as well as lack skill at planning their written work, place unnecessary demands on a teacher's time and attention. This section offers strategies to help these students stay organized and to keep them from creating disorganization discord.

Remember John Hancock
for Younger Students

A teacher is preparing to collect arithmetic tests from her third grade class. "All right everyone," she directs them. "Put your pencils down please. Take out a highlight marker and highlight your name. If you don't have a highlighter, underline your name with your favorite colored crayon."

The students quickly locate their markers and highlight their names. A few giggle nervously and reach for their pencils as they realize that they have failed to put their names on their papers.

(What It Is:) *Remember John Hancock for Younger Students* is a memory-prodding motivational technique, which also teaches students about one of our Founding Fathers. It gently reminds students to write their names on their papers.

(Why It's Used:) In their enthusiasm to begin an assignment, younger students frequently forget to write their names on their papers. These nameless papers often create classroom chaos when the teacher returns graded work to the class. Protests such as, "I didn't get my paper back! Where's mine? I didn't get mine!" are voiced along with, depending on the age and sensitivity of the students, weeping and gnashing of teeth. *Remember John Hancock* helps prevent such unpleasant scenarios by encouraging students to check to see if they have put their names on their work.

(How It's Done:) Give your students (or ask that they supply) a highlight marker. Direct them at either the beginning or end of a written assignment to highlight their names.

(Perils and Pitfalls:) Students can get carried away and highlight a great deal more than just their names or they sometimes use a dark-colored regular marker instead of a highlighter to "highlight" their names. Avoid overly decorative embellishments and name obscuring marker choices by stressing that only names should be highlighted and assigning a certain color highlighter for name highlighting only. For example, only yellow can be used to highlight a name, therefore, yellow can only appear once on a paper.

Variations on a Theme:

- In lieu of using the highlighting procedure, establish a bell-ringing procedure. Procure a small dinner bell. Select one student each day to be the "name-reminder-ringer." Have that student ring the bell as a reminder to students to put their names on their papers.

Remember John Hancock
for Older Students

A teacher is returning graded test papers to his eighth-grade class. He finishes calling students' names but still has papers that have not been returned to students.

Three students wave their hands in the air. "I didn't get my test paper back," says one.

"Me either!" chorus the other two.

"Well, guys, I have three papers here without names. I guess they must be yours, but since they don't have any names on them, I don't know which paper belongs to whom. So you three have a choice. You can either take a zero grade for this test or you can take a makeup test."

All three students ponder the possibilities and reluctantly decide to complete a makeup test. As the teacher hands the new test papers to the students he says, "Now, guys, what is the first and most important piece of information you must remember to put on your paper?"

(What It Is:) *Remember John Hancock for Older Students* is a behavior modification technique. It compels students to identify their work and demonstrates that inattention to seemingly minor details can cause unpleasant consequences.

(Why It's Used:) In their rush to begin an assignment students frequently forget to write their names on their papers. *Remember John Hancock* reinforces the importance of completing this small yet extremely important detail by confronting them with difficult choices if they fail to do so. It affords the owners of nameless papers an opportunity to make amends for their careless mistake (should they choose to do so) and helps reduce counterproductive outbursts of anger and complaints of unfairness that result from implementing the standard operating procedure of placing nameless papers handed in by older students in the circular file (a.k.a. trash can).

(How It's Done:) Discuss with your class the importance of paying attention to seemingly minor details and the problems that result when people fail to do so. (For example: lug nuts not tightened can cause the wheel to fall off of a car and result in a serious accident, or a stove burner left on can result in a house fire.) Explain that their omission of the seemingly minor detail of writing their names on their papers will result in serious consequences for them.

(Perils and Pitfalls:) Students will sometimes attempt to identify their nameless paper and convince you to accept it. Negate this behavior by refusing to make nameless papers available for student review until after they have completed the makeup test or agreed to take a zero grade for the test.

Parents may object to what they perceive as a needlessly harsh consequence for an unintentional lapse in attention on the part of their child. Prevent these objections by carefully explaining your policy regarding nameless papers in guidelines distributed to students at the beginning of the school year, reiterating those guidelines during parent-teacher conferences, and justifying the need for them.

(Variations on a Theme:)
- In lieu of administering and grading a makeup test, allow students to identify their test papers (if the test format makes positive identification possible) and deduct a substantial number of points from each student's test grade.

Just Scrap It Writing

As a culminating activity for a unit on American Heroes, a fifth-grade remedial reading teacher tells his students to write a paragraph of at least five sentences about any hero they have studied. The class groans and the teacher says, "Come on, guys, it's not that hard to write a five-sentence paragraph."

A tall boy whispers, "Maybe it's easy for you, but it isn't easy for us!"

"Why, Murray?" asks the teacher. "I'm serious. What makes it hard for you?"

"It's hard 'cause I know what I want to say, but I can't get it down right and when I finally do, you teachers mark it all up and tell me to write it over. Man, I hate this stuff!"

"Okay, Murray, I get your point. How about we try a little different way of doing this?"

The teacher grabs a stack of 8½-by-11-inch scrap paper and folds and tears it into quarters. He hands the torn paper to Murray and tells him to give everyone in the class six or seven pieces. When everyone has a small supply of scrap paper, he says to the class, "I'm going to ask you a question and also write it on the board. I want you to take one piece of scrap paper and write the answer to my question in a sentence. Your sentence will be easier to write if you put some of the words from my question in it. That's why I'm writing the question on the board, so you can see the words." He then asks and writes, "What American hero is your paragraph about?" When it appears that almost everyone in the class has finished, he says, "Okay, Murray, you're on! Read your answer for us."

Murray says, "Aw, man, this is too simple!" and then reads, "This paragraph is about Arthur Ashe."

"Good job, Murray. You follow directions well and are off to a good start."

The teacher calls on other students who share slightly different versions of the same sentence. He then directs his students to put a large number one on the back of the scrap paper they have written on.

"Now we're ready for question number two," he says. "Everyone grab another piece of scrap paper and answer this question: 'What did this person do to become a hero?'"

The teacher again checks with students as they write, calls on students to share their answers, and this time has them place the number two on the back of their scrap. He repeats the procedure of asking simplified direct questions and having students write each response on a separate piece of scrap paper until they have written five sentences on five pieces of numbered scrap paper. He then says to the class, "Well, that's it, guys. You've written a first draft of your paragraph on an American hero. Now all you have to do is copy what you've written in the correct order on a sheet of composition paper or key it in on the computer."

"Man, I think we been had . . . 'cause that wasn't too bad!" raps Murray, causing the class to break into laughter.

"It ain't hard to do . . . when you just think it through!" counter-raps the teacher, causing even greater laughter.

(**What It Is:**) *Just Scrap It Writing* is an organizational and motivational procedure. It helps students organize their thoughts, relieves their anxiety about putting their thoughts into writing, and overcomes their reluctance to revise and rewrite compositions.

(**Why It's Used:**) Students often struggle to write a composition on an assigned topic because they don't know where to begin, they fear making mistakes, and dread the rewriting process. *Just Scrap It Writing* teaches them to begin by asking basic questions. It helps them overcome their fear of making mistakes and their dread of rewriting by concretely illustrating that the initial stage of formulating and organizing their ideas consists of just putting their thoughts in writing. It reinforces through concrete example the basic structure of an introductory paragraph.

How It's Done: Tear 8½-by-11-inch newsprint or scrap paper into fourths. Distribute a handful of the torn paper to each student. Ask a brief and precise question. Jot the question on the board or other visual display. Direct your students to write a sentence that answers the question on one of their pieces of scrap paper and to number the paper to correspond with the number of your question. Call on a few students to share their answers. Continue this procedure until your students have enough material to write a paragraph. Have students write a good draft of their composition by copying the sentences they have written onto composition paper or into a computer.

Perils and Pitfalls: When a lesson using *Just Scrap It Writing* requires more than one teaching period to complete, the collection and subsequent return of all pertinent scrap pieces can create confusion. This is especially true if numerous scrap pieces are missing their owners' names. It's imperative, therefore, that students put their names or, at the very least, their initials on each piece of paper, that they clip their scrap pieces together securely, and that all materials then be collected and returned in an organized fashion.

Students with poor reading and writing skills may write answers of only one or two words. One way to address this is to have them include key words from a question in their answer statement.

Variations on a Theme:

- Distribute several sheets of blank paper and have students make their own scrap.

- Challenge students who finish more quickly than the rest to jot down on an extra piece of scrap their prediction of your next question.

- Have students add supporting information to their basic paragraphs by adding scrap pieces or have them reorganize their paragraphs by changing the order of their scrap pieces.

The Right Questions Can Help Your Students Write Sentences for Answers

When using Just Scrap It Writing *you can encourage students to answer in sentences by carefully crafting questions so they are comprised of key words that your less-skilled students can incorporate into their answer statements. For example, a question worded, "What is the title of the book you read?" can be answered by writing the sentence, "The title of the book I read is* A Taste of Blackberries;*" the question, "Who is the author?" can be answered by writing, "The author is Doris Smith;" the question, "What is the first significant event that happens in this book?" can be answered by writing, "The first significant event that happens in this book is ____."*

All of these questions are worded to provide students with poor writing skills the basic framework to answer in sentences and sequenced to help them form those sentences into a simple paragraph.

Create key-word questions using simple who, what, when, where, why, and how interrogatives. Keep the questions straightforward and logically sequential. Then attempt to use the key words in your questions to write basic statement answers. Should you find this difficult to accomplish, your questions must be revised using less-complicated wording structures and if possible, more perceptible key words. An example of an essay-test question that definitely needs revision would be, "American pioneers suffered many hardships during their travels to what is now California. Describe three of those hardships and explain how the pioneers overcame them." This question might be revised to read, "What were three hardships that American pioneers suffered as they traveled to California? How did the pioneers overcome these hardships?"

Just Scrap It Practice

A teacher is explaining how to determine through deduction and calculation the missing pieces of perimeter measurement of an L-shaped geometric figure. She demonstrates the process to the class, and calls on student volunteers to solve problems at the board and explain their solutions. A few students understand the deductive calculation process and apply it correctly; however, there are several who seem somewhat tentative and confused. "Does everyone understand how James got the missing measurement for the base of the L-shaped geometric figure? He added together the perimeter measurements that were given for the top two pieces of the upright L," says the teacher. She looks around the room and asks "Does anyone have any questions?"

Several students shake their heads, "no."

"Okay then," she says apprehensively. "I guess you're ready to try to find some mystery perimeters on your own."

She distributes practice sheets to the class and students begin working on them. After a few minutes, however, several students raise their hands.

"I can't figure this out," says one student. "There aren't enough numbers here for me to work with."

"Me either!" exclaims another.

"I need you to show me how to do that adding and subtracting thing again," says a third.

"I can't do this stuff! I just don't get it!" sighs another.

The exasperated and overwhelmed teacher realizes that her class needs more instruction and practice before they can complete the independent work she has mistakenly assigned. She stops her students and tells them to put their practice sheets away. She then gives each student a small stack of scrap pieces, writes a problem on the board, directs everyone to copy it on one of their pieces of scrap, and walks them through the solution, making sure they complete the work on their scrap as she models it at the board. She repeats this procedure several times, directing her students to use a fresh scrap piece for each solution. Next, she writes a problem on the board, has her students copy it on a fresh sheet of scrap, directs them to complete it independently, travels around the room to observe what they are actually writing on their scrap pieces, and, after a reasonable period of time, walks them through the solution. When the class has solved several problems on scrap pieces correctly and appears to have a better grasp of the theorem, the teacher directs them to begin work once again on their independent practice sheets.

(What It Is:) *Just Scrap It Practice* is a teacher-directed review, reinforcement, and informal assessment procedure. It increases students' understanding of newly introduced concepts and reduces their frustration levels when trying to master those concepts.

(Why It's Used:) When teaching a new concept, teachers generally present the concept, choose students who appear to understand it to model its correct use for the class, and assign an independent practice exercise for reinforcement. Often, however, students need extra teacher-directed practice to help them understand the new concept's application before they can complete independent practice exercises successfully. *Just Scrap It Practice*, with its fresh start for each new problem and concrete it's-okay-to-make-a-mistake-message (a new piece of paper that's scrapped after each solution) provides this practice in a fail-safe fashion.

(How It's Done:) Preparation for *Just Scrap It Practice* is the same as that for *Just Scrap It Writing.* Simply tear 8½-by-11-inch scrap paper or blank newsprint into fourths and distribute a handful of the torn paper to each student. In lieu of the questioning and sentence-writing procedure used in *Just Scrap It Writing*, however, write a problem on the board, transparency, or other means of display, direct your students to copy the problem on a piece of their scrap, and have them work along with you as you solve the problem. After they have solved a few practice problems in this manner, have them copy and solve a problem independently, and call on students to share their answers. Continue this procedure until it appears that the majority understands the new concept well enough to apply it without the need for help. Then, distribute a set of practice exercises for students to complete independently.

(**Perils and Pitfalls:**) Students who are still having difficulty understanding a concept after being "walked" through it step-by-step several times may simply "go through the motions" of problem solving when told to solve a *Just Scrap It Practice* problem independently. Prevent this from happening by carefully observing the work of students who seem to be struggling.

Students who quickly master the concept can become bored with the restrictiveness of the step-by-step procedure. Program for these students by placing a "bonus problem challenge" on the board to be completed by anyone who finishes the assigned problem before it is checked, or if the students in your class get along well together, allow those who really do understand the concept to tutor those who need additional help.

Use of *Just Scrap It Practice* can leave a classroom in scrap paper shambles and subject to surreptitious paper wad wars when all waste pieces are not collected promptly. Therefore, a definite system for trash collection and disposal when using this technique is a must.

(**Variations on a Theme:**)
- Have students create and solve their own scrap problems and after doing so, give them to their neighbors to solve. When using this variation, be sure your students understand that the problems they create are to be modeled after those they have completed for practice.

Contents List Procrastination Preventive

It's the last ten minutes of a Social Studies class. The teacher directs her students to clear everything from their desks. She then says, "You all know that the contents list for your long-term Social Studies research report is due next Monday. I just want to make sure everyone is clear about the contents list and what you are to include in it. The contents list," she continues, "is a list of the important points you will cover in your report, in the order in which you will report on them. For each point you must cite at least two sources that you have found with information about that point. Is everyone clear on this? Does anyone have any questions?"

A student seated near the door raises his hand tentatively. "I'm not sure what the contents list is supposed to be. Is it like an outline?"

"In a way it's like an outline," answers the teacher, "but it's easier to write than an outline because it doesn't require you to list subheadings and lots of supporting details the way an outline does."

Another student raises her hand and complains, "I don't see why we have to do a contents list and put down our sources and stuff. Why can't we just write our report and hand it in for a grade?"

"Actually your approach would be easier for everyone, Lisa," replies the teacher, "but unfortunately, easier isn't always better. Without some incentive to help them get started, too many students wait until the last minute to begin work on their report and then they get a poor grade because they don't have the time to do a good job. By requiring you to hand in a contents list, I can make sure you are beginning to work on your report in time to do a good job."

(**What It Is:**) Contents List Procrastination Preventive is a technique that compels students to spend time working on research projects. It requires students to hand in a contents list for their research project well ahead of the paper's final due date.

(**Why It's Used:**) Students frequently put off researching a paper until it is too late for them to do the necessary research. *Contents List Procrastination Preventive* compels them to focus on and complete preliminary research on a project several days before it is due. Also, a contents list submission requirement is more helpful to less-capable students than is a requirement that they submit a preliminary outline since these students often find the outlining task itself bewildering and overwhelming.

Sound **Advice**

Sample Contents List

Topic: The Battle of Baltimore and the History of the Star-Spangled Banner

1. British war ships anchor near Fort McHenry.

    a. SOURCE _____

    b. SOURCE _____

2. Francis Scott Key held prisoner on a British ship.

    a. SOURCE _____

    b. SOURCE _____

3. British ships bombard Fort McHenry.

    a. SOURCE _____

    b. SOURCE _____

4. The Americans at Fort McHenry fight off the British.

    a. SOURCE _____

    b. SOURCE _____

5. Francis Scott Key writes the Star-Spangled Banner.

    a. SOURCE _____

    b. SOURCE _____

(How It's Done:) When assigning a research paper, direct your students to submit a contents list several days before the completed paper's due date. Review the submissions and discuss any possible problem areas with them.

(Perils and Pitfalls:) Vague contents list entries or lists unrelated to the research paper contents can cause students serious problems when they begin writing their papers. Prevent this by requiring that each entry refer to material specifically contained in that part of the report. For example, a section with the general title "Thomas Jefferson" might instead be more specifically entitled "How Thomas Jefferson Helped Write the Declaration of Independence."

(Variations on a Theme:)

- Allow students who are more comfortable writing an outline the choice of submitting an outline in lieu of a table of contents.

- Have students submit the first page as well as the table of contents as a way of encouraging them to get started in the writing process.

Notebook Model

A teacher is distributing handout notes to his class. He tells his students to place the page in the Class Notes section of their Social Studies notebook directly after the notes they had taken the previous day. As he does so, he takes from the chalk ledge at the front of the classroom a large prominently displayed loose-leaf notebook filled with pages and dividers, holds it in the air for everyone to see, demonstrates exactly where the page is to be placed, and waits for the class to follow his directions.

A student seated near the back of the room says, "Mr. James, I think I'm missing a vocabulary list that you gave the class the day I was absent."

"Well, Mary," replies the teacher. "Check the class notebook and let me know which sheet you are missing, and I'll give you one. The same goes for anyone else who thinks they're missing notes. Just remember, if they are notes that I made and gave to you and you lost them, I won't give you another copy. If you lost your notes, it's your responsibility to make new ones."

(What It Is:) *Notebook Model* is a structuring technique. It helps students maintain an organized notebook.

(Why It's Used:) Poorly organized students seldom do well in school, and their teachers are always searching for techniques to help them get and stay organized. One simple organizing technique is to maintain and constantly refer to a model notebook.

(How It's Done:) Obtain a large loose-leaf notebook. Organize and maintain it as a model for your students. Display it prominently in your classroom and ensure that your students have access to it as a reference.

(Perils and Pitfalls:) Notebook models can mysteriously disappear from classrooms, as can important and lengthy pages from those models. Thwart these disappearances by conspicuously marking the notebook and each note page with the word MODEL (or a similar word such as SAMPLE), or if time and your school budget allows, you can laminate the model notebook pages.

Variations on a Theme:

- Instead of maintaining the notebook model yourself, have students with well-organized notebooks take responsibility for this task.

- Make the job of "notebook coordinator" a special honor and use it as an incentive for students to keep organized notebooks.

Color Coded Work Folders

It is the beginning of the school year and a second-grade class is transitioning from their reading lesson to their math lesson.

"Boys and girls, everyone, eyes on me," their teacher says. She waits patiently for their attention. "We have just finished our reading lesson for today. Somebody raise their hand and tell me where we are going to put our reading papers."

Several students wave their hands in the air excitedly, and the teacher nods to one. "Yes, Eddie, where do we put our reading papers?"

"Our reading papers go in our red folders," says Eddie.

"That's right, Eddie. Red folders are for reading and only reading papers are to be put in red folders," reiterates the teacher. "Everyone take out your red folder and place your reading paper inside it." The teacher watches carefully as her students search through their desks, take out their red folders, and place their reading papers inside of them. She then points to the day's schedule printed on the board and says, "Our next subject today is math. Now take out your math folder and look inside it to find yesterday's math paper." She waits patiently for her students to locate their math folders and find their yesterday's math papers. She then asks, "What color folder should I see on everyone's desk?"

"Green!" answers the class in unison.

"Good job!" replies the teacher. "Listen carefully because I'm going to ask you a long question. Who can tell me what other color folders you have in your desk that we haven't used today and what subjects they are for?"

Three children raise their hands to answer. "Yes, Marcie, can you remember all of my long question and give me an answer to it?" asks the teacher.

"I have a yellow folder and a blue folder in my desk that I haven't used today." answers Marcie.

"And papers from what subjects are put in these folders, Marcie?" prompts the teacher.

"We put science papers in the yellow folder and social studies papers in the blue folder." answers Marcie confidently.

(What It Is:) *Color Coded Work Folders* is a method of keeping students' work organized. It teaches students one way to arrange their work for easy access and can help them transition to organizational strategies using words instead of colors.

(Why It's Used:) Young students, as well as older students with poor study skills, must learn to keep their schoolwork organized. One of the easiest ways to help them learn this is to have them use color-coded work folders.

(How It's Done:) Obtain a supply of two-pocket folders in a variety of colors. (Some teachers place these on the list of required school supplies to be purchased by parents, some use discretionary funds provided by the PTA to purchase folders, and some simply make their own by folding colored construction paper.) Distribute the folders to your students. Decide on a color to be used for each subject. Have your students label each folder with the name of the subject for which it will be used as well as their own name. Direct them to place their work in the correct folder when necessary.

(Perils and Pitfalls:) Sometimes students, especially those who are poorly organized, take their folders home and forget to bring them back to school the next day. This can cause them to be without essential classwork material from the previous day. A solution to this problem is to issue a separate folder for homework and at the end of the school day remind students that they may take home only their homework folders.

(Variations on a Theme:)
- As the year progresses allow each student to decide which color he or she wants to use for each subject folder. Be aware,

however, that while this variation gives your students control over which colors they want to use for each subject folder, you can no longer easily monitor the correctness of the folder they have on their desks nor can you direct the entire class to locate a subject folder by color instead of by name.

Have Question, Will Travel

It's lunchtime and a third-grade class is traveling in line from their class-room to the cafeteria. As they move through the hall, the teacher says quietly, "Mavis, tell us the product of three times three."

Mavis smiles and says, "That's an easy one! It's nine."

"Jordan, how about three times five?"

Jordan shakes his head.

"Can you help your buddy Jordan out, Jamal?"

"It's . . . five . . . ten . . . fifteen," calculates Jamal. "It's fifteen," he says confidently.

This low-keyed traveling review of multiplication facts continues until the class arrives at the cafeteria and is dismissed for lunch.

What It Is: *Have Question, Will Travel* is an informal review and reinforcement procedure. It helps keep students focused and organized in loosely structured settings such as when they are in line before and after lunch, going to and coming from recess, and traveling to and from special area subjects.

Why It's Used: At times when classes travel from place to place in line, the spaces between students tend to stretch long distances and inappropriate student interactions occur. *Have Question, Will Travel* helps prevent such problems by constructively focusing students as they travel.

How It's Done: Explain the procedure and your expectations for how it is to be carried out before your students leave the classroom. This can usually be accomplished while the class is in line in your classroom. If, however, your class is an unusually loquacious group, it may be best to explain the procedure before they are standing in line.

Sound Advice

Example of an Introductory Dialogue

Teacher: *"All right, everyone, listen up. We're going to try something different on the way to the gym for physical education today. We're going to play* Have Question, Will Travel."

Nearby student: *"What's that?"*

Teacher: *"It's when I challenge everyone to answer some review questions as we travel through the halls."*

Another nearby student: *"But I thought we're not supposed to talk while we're in line?'*

Teacher: *"You're absolutely right, José, but that's part of the challenge. You know that we're not supposed to disturb other classes as we move through the halls, so in order for us not to do that, I have to ask the question very quietly and someone has to answer it very quietly."*

Third student: *"What's the rest of the challenge?"*

Teacher: *"Well, the real challenge is to see how many questions you can answer correctly during a traveling review. We'll keep score each time we do a traveling review and see if we can break our own record. Who'd like to be today's scorekeeper?" (Several hands wave in the air.) "Okay, Estephanie, you can be the official scorekeeper for today."*

"Now, let's try out a practice question right here in the classroom. Everyone face forward just like when we travel in line and listen carefully because you know I have to speak quietly." (A student quietly answers the practice question and the class begins their journey to the gym answering traveling review questions as they do so.)

(**Perils and Pitfalls:**) Students can become boisterous to the point of disturbing nearby classes or distracted so that they bump into one another during a particularly engaging traveling review. Avoid boisterousness by insisting that your students speak softly out of respect for classes that are in session. Prevent accidental student collisions by accepting answers only once the class has stopped moving and asking a new question before the class begins moving again. This compels students to ponder answers while they are traveling and share them when they are standing still.

(**Variations on a Theme:**)

- Use *Have Question, Will Travel* whenever extended periods of down time begin to wreak havoc on your students' self control, such as an unusually long wait before the beginning of an assembly or during long field-trip bus rides. During bus trips, however, it's best to ask some "fun" questions about current culture, like "What are the names of three rap artists whose first names begin with an 'S'?" in addition to curriculum review questions.

- Have students pose their own questions for the traveling review with the stipulation that they must know the correct answer to any question they ask.

Visit from Inspector Clouseau

A first-grade class has just returned from lunch. As the students go to their desks, a small girl exclaims, "The Desk Inspector was here, and I got a Neat and Orderly Desk Award!"

"Me, too!" exclaims another child as the rest of the children rush to their desks to see if they also received Neat and Orderly Desk Awards from the Desk Inspector.

What It Is: *Visit from Inspector Clouseau* is a motivational technique to help students keep their desk areas neat and orderly.

Why It's Used: For the sake of classroom organization and positive esthetics, teachers find themselves frequently reminding their messier students to keep their desks and surrounding areas neat and orderly. *Visit from Inspector Clouseau* is a fun way to reinforce desirable organizational habits.

How It's Done: Purchase (or use a computer to design and print) certificates to be used for Neat and Orderly Desk Awards. Early in the school year tell your class that during the year the Desk Inspector will visit their classroom by surprise to see if their desks and the areas near them are neat and orderly. Explain that when the Inspector finds a student's desk that is really neat and orderly, he leaves a Neat and Orderly Desk Award on that student's desk. Place a certificate on display in the classroom. Allow a few days to pass, and have *Inspector Clouseau* make a surprise visit.

Perils and Pitfalls: Some students become very upset when they fail to earn a Neat and Orderly Desk Award. Allow them time to calm down and then point out the differences between the orderliness in their areas and the orderliness in the areas of those who received awards.

Variations on a Theme:

- In the interest of objectivity, have someone other than yourself be *Inspector Clouseau*.

- In lieu of or in addition to a certificate give a small treat to those with neat and orderly desks.

- Keep a tally of the number of certificates each child earns during the school year and give a special award to the child who earns the most.

Part IV

Positively Perfect

Strategies That Build Self-Esteem and Create a Positive Learning Environment

A Lesson in the Power of Positive Teaching

"We already got rid of one teacher this year, and we can get rid of you!" proclaimed the young man seated near the back of the classroom.

"Great, just great! Why in the world did I ever agree to do this?" I thought as I entered the classroom.

Only the week before I had been seated in my principal's office listening to ego-inflating compliments about my "extraordinary teaching skills" and allowing myself to be flattered into taking on a "troublesome" class whose teacher had quit out of exasperation.

"These kids need structure," my principal had said. "They run roughshod over their teachers, fight with one another almost constantly, do very little academically, and view themselves as the worst class in the school, a view that, unfortunately, is shared by many others in this building. They need an experienced teacher to help them turn things around so they can get an education and feel good about themselves."

So I agreed to teach an exceptionally difficult class and was soon working determinedly to change a negative classroom environment into a positive one. I calmly ignored their rude greetings, presented my new charges with age-appropriate behavioral guidelines, and patiently and consistently demanded that they be followed on a daily basis. Next, I planned and implemented lessons such as *Caught You Doing The Right Thing* and *My Life in Collage* to address their need for fun and freedom as well as structure and control. Finally, I employed activities designed to build their self esteem, including the *Compliment a Classmate Draw*, and *Guess That Student*. Instead of improving over the first week or so, however, my students' behavior worsened (as though that were possible). Having little recourse and much experience working with "challenging" students, I hung in there tenaciously and waited for them to realize that I wasn't going to give up and go home. Then slowly, almost imperceptibly at first, the atmosphere in the classroom began to change. My students stopped laughing when someone made a rude comment or a mistake. They no longer squabbled among themselves, but asked if we could have a meeting to discuss the problem. They began to willingly participate in activities designed to build their confidence, and they started to listen more attentively when their classmates were talking.

By the end of the school year the class was by no means the epitome of behavioral perfection but their behavior was improved and they had made measurable academic progress. More importantly, they no longer viewed school as a terrible place where they seldom met with success, but instead, saw it as a place where they could, with some effort and concessions, be as successful as everyone else.

A Word About Positively Perfect

The classroom environment has a huge impact on learning. Classrooms with negative environments are stressful, joyless places where much valuable teaching time is wasted on petty bickering, name calling, finger pointing, tattling, and rule enforcement. Such places generate terribly negative feelings that hinder the learning process. The teacher's challenge is to create a learning environment that decisively diminishes the negative and plausibly stresses the positive. The strategies in this section are designed to help you create such an environment.

My Life in Collage

It is the end of the first week of school and in one classroom the teacher and a student are standing together at the front of a classroom. The student holds a tag-board collage entitled, "All About Me," as the teacher says, "We've already noted that Todd's collage has a picture of three boys, a German Shepherd, and a mountain bike, and correctly concluded that he has two brothers, a German Shepherd, and a mountain bike. Do you have any questions for Todd about these items?" says the teacher.

Several students raise their hands, and the teacher continues, "Well, Todd, it looks like your collage has triggered some interest. Why don't you call on someone? And remember if someone asks you a question that you don't want to answer, simply tell them you'd prefer not to answer it."

Todd points to a student with his hand raised, "What's your dog's name and how old is he?"

Todd giggles and says, "My dog's name is Moochie, and she's five."

The students ask Todd questions about his dog, his brothers, and his dirt bike. The teacher stops them by asking, "Okay, class, what other things do you see in Todd's collage, and what do you think they might tell us about him?"

"There's a picture of a guy snowboarding," ventures a student, "so maybe Todd likes to snowboard?"

"What about it, Todd? asks the teacher. "Do you like to snowboard?"

"No," answers Todd with a shy grin. "I put that in my collage 'cause you told us to include our goals in our collage and one of my goals is to learn how to snowboard."

"Okay, Todd," continues the teacher, "now that we've examined and thought about your collage a bit, why don't you tell us why the rest of the items you included are important to you?"

What It Is: *My Life in Collage* is a way for students to learn about their classmates. It provides a creative visual tool for speakers and listeners when students are asked to tell about themselves and their interests.

Why It's Used: It introduces students to one another and helps them discover their mutual interests.

How It's Done: Create a collage about yourself. Share this with your students and discuss the meaning of the items in your collage. (Once you have completed your first collage lesson, you may have a few *My Life in Collages* from the previous year to show as examples and you might also want to laminate your personal *My Life in Collage* to preserve it for future use.) Allow "think time" for your students to jot down some ideas about the kinds of items they want to put in their collage. If this is an in-school assignment, make available the materials necessary for creating a collage, such as tag board, pictographic magazines and newspapers, scissors, paste, and crayons. If this is a homework assignment, be certain your students have these materials available to them at home. Allow appropriate work time and assist students as needed. Have students share and discuss their collages with the class. (Review introductory scenario to this strategy for a sample discussion.)

Perils and Pitfalls: Sometimes students, without their parents' permission, include priceless family photos and memorabilia in their collages, causing irreparable damage to these items. Prevent this from happening by stressing to your students that they are not to use any family photos or special family items such as ticket stubs from past sporting events, awards certificates, or celebrity autographs without their parents' permission.

Also, since collage creation is a loosely structured enjoyable activity, it can easily turn into a time-consuming one with students pouring through magazines looking for "just the right picture." Therefore, whether the collages are to be done in class or at home, be sure to set and adhere to strict time limit guidelines for their completion and, for those activities that don't lend themselves well to magazine pictures, consider allowing students to add a few of their own drawings to their collages.

Variations on a Theme:

1. Keep a *My Life in Collage* creation kit tucked away in the corner of a closet for use with new students.

2. Poll the class for general common interests, group students accordingly, and have each group create a collage highlighting their special interest (for example: football, cooking, pets, camping, etc.).

3. Have older students complete a "career interest collage" consisting of pictures related to a career they might want to pursue in the future.

Negative to Positive Parry

It's the end of lunch period when a very angry fifth grader approaches the teacher.

"The cafeteria monitor yelled at me and made me sit at the Quiet Table for talking too loud when I wasn't even talking! She's so mean! Everybody hates her!"

"Now, Jennifer," the teacher responds calmly, "I know you're very upset because you feel the cafeteria monitor treated you unfairly, but what is it that you must do before I can help you with your problem?"

"I know! I know! I'm supposed to tell you something good about what happened, but nothing good happened!"

"Listen, Jen, I've taught you for several months now and I know you have a good head on your shoulders, so I know that you can find something good to say about what happened. You just have to stop thinking about what went wrong during lunch today and start thinking about what went right."

"Well," Jennifer replies haltingly. "I did get to spend most of my lunch period with my friends 'cause Miss Mary only made me sit at the Quiet Table for five minutes and today was pizza day and I love pizza!"

"There you go! You did it! You found some good in something bad that happened to you! So how about, after everyone gets working on their independent assignment, we get together and spend a few minutes talking about what happened?"

"Okay, but I still think Miss Mary is mean even if she did send me to the Quiet Table for only five minutes."

(**What It Is:**) *Negative to Positive Parry* is a strategy that helps assuage angry students. It helps students focus on the positive rather than fuming over the negative.

(**Why It's Used:**) Students who are angry because they view ordinary daily admonishments as affronts to their self esteem often cause classroom behavior problems. When employed carefully, *Negative to Positive Parry* calms these angry students and teaches them to view negative events more positively.

(**How It's Done:**) Explain *Negative to Positive Parry* to your students before the need for its use arises. Introduce it during a class discussion on appropriate ways to handle problems and complaints. Present the concept that most life events have both positive and negative ramifications, practice finding the positive in some likely school-related negative scenarios, and role-play the approach's use. After your students understand *Negative to Positive Parry* and have practiced its use, encourage them to use it when appropriate.

(**Perils and Pitfalls:**) *Negative to Positive Parry* does not work with outraged students. Give these young people a cooling-off period of ten or twenty minutes before attempting to use it. Then attempt to employ the technique in a low-key and reasonable manner. However, should irate students mock your efforts by making comments such as, "I guess you want me to be happy, happy, happy right now!" or, "I'm not going to say anything good about Mr. Larson and you're not going to make me, so get out of my face!" calmly tell them that it's indeed their choice to view things negatively and remain angry if they wish. Remind them you are offering them a way to get over their anger and enjoy the rest of their day. Then back off and let the matter rest.

(**Variations on a Theme:**)

- During down time at the end of the school day help students to focus on the positive by asking them to tell you five good things that happened that day.

- At the end of the week list on the board, transparency, or computer display screen several positive things that happened that week.

Example of a Class Discussion to Introduce Negative to Positive Parry

Teacher: "Okay, everyone, you've suggested some really helpful ways to handle problems and complaints. Now I want to talk with you about another way, but before I do, I'm going to ask you to think about snow and tell me some good things that happen when it snows." *(The teacher accepts several answers from students and lists them on the board.)*

Teacher: "Okay, now I want you to reverse course and tell me some bad things that happen when it snows!" *(The teacher again accepts several answers and lists them on the board.)*

Teacher: "Everyone take a look at the two lists that we made. What do you notice about our lists?"

First Student: "It looks like we found just as many good things as bad things about snow."

Teacher: "And? Anything else about when you compare the good and bad things?"

Second Student: "The good and bad things are just the opposite of each other."

Teacher: "What do you mean by the opposite of each other?"

Second Student: "Well, for instance, when it snows really heavy, school closes and we get the day off and to us, that's good. But when school closes, we have to give up some of our vacation days to make up the days missed, and that's bad."

Teacher: "Good observation, but does it hold true for most of our list?" *(The teacher reinforces the point by accepting several more student comparisons.)*

Teacher: "I guess we could say, 'Snow is just snow. Whether we see it as good or bad really just depends on us.' So what does this discussion about snow have to do with another way you can deal with problems? Well, guys, you can look at any situation the way we

(continued on next page)

98

looked at snow. We can view it as good or positive as well as bad or negative, and sometimes when we're upset and angry it's best for us to try to see the positive. Who can give me an example of something a student might get in trouble for?" (Almost every student in the room volunteers to answer.)

Student: *"Listening to a Walkman in school."*

Teacher: *"So a student is traveling through the halls listening to a Walkman when he's reprimanded by a teacher. The teacher says, 'Young Man, please take that Walkman off and put it away or it will become mine until your parents come to school to get it.' In what ways does the student view this situation as negative?"*

(Students reply with such answers as, "He won't be able to listen to his favorite music," and, "The teacher is on a power trip and ought to just chill out and mind her own business.")

Teacher: *"Now here's the challenging part, what are some ways the student can view the situation as good, or at least not so bad?"*

First Student: *"Well, he could think, 'At least the teacher just warned me and didn't ask me to give up my Walkman.'"*

Teacher: *"Very good, Gillian! It looks like you've caught on quickly. Is someone else brave enough to give it a try?"*

Second Student: *"Or he might realize that if every kid in the school was walking around listening to a Walkman, we'd all be bumping into one another and missing emergency announcements and stuff."*

Teacher: *"All right, I think you see that our hypothetical student can view the Walkman incident as not just negative, but also, at least to some degree, positive. I want you to understand that when dealing with problems, it's wise to focus on the positive and not just the negative."*

Caught You Doing the Right Thing

A student with an armful of books is hurrying through a crowded hallway on the way to her next class. Her notebook binder slips from her arms and crashes to the floor, scattering its contents everywhere. As she tries to gather up all of her materials, two students stop to help her. As they hand her the last of her notebook pages, a smiling teacher appears, hands each of the Good Samaritans a slip of paper, and says, "Caught you doing the right thing!"

"All right! This is my third Caught You slip today! Dude, I'm on a roll! Just one more and I'll lead my class and get to go to the Caught You Doing the Right Thing Party!" exclaims one of the pleased recipients as he heads for his next class.

(What It Is:) *Caught You Doing the Right Thing* is a behavior modification technique. It rewards students for appropriate behavior.

(Why It's Used:) It improves student conduct by tangibly reinforcing positive behavior.

(How It's Done:)

1. Determine the specific behaviors you wish to reinforce (for example, thoughtfulness to others, acceptable hall conduct, use of appropriate language, etc.) and the period of time over which they will be reinforced.

2. Think of some possible rewards for those who collect the most tokens or brainstorm some possible rewards with your students once you introduce the contest to the class.

3. Construct paper tokens to use for immediate tangible reinforcement.

4. Introduce the *Caught You Doing the Right Thing* contest to your students during a class discussion about good manners and appropriate behavior. Stress the many positive behaviors you see your students display and then mention there are areas

that could still use some improvement. Describe these for the class (they might be, for example, politeness in the cafeteria, patience when waiting to get on the school bus, speaking softly in the halls, etc.) and present the *Caught You Doing the Right Thing* contest as a fun way to help them improve their behavior in those areas. Distribute a *Caught You Doing the Right Thing* paper token to each student. Explain that whenever you catch a student doing the right thing, you will give him or her a paper token, and students who collect the greatest number of tokens during the *Caught You Doing the Right Thing* contest period will earn a reward.

5. If you wish to reinforce your students' behavior outside of your classroom, review the *Caught You Doing the Right Thing* procedure with school staff members who agree to participate. Give them a handful of paper tokens to issue to your students when they catch them doing the right thing.

6. Encourage enthusiastic student participation at the beginning of the contest by generously reinforcing the targeted behaviors.

(**Perils and Pitfalls:**) As with all competitive activities, *Caught You Doing the Right Thing* is subject to cheating. Students can pilfer tokens or coerce less competitive students into "donating" their tokens to them. Reduce the likelihood of such dishonesty by developing guidelines that instruct students to write their names on their tokens and warn them of disqualification should they donate their tokens to (or accept donated tokens from) others. Also, angry students who feel they earned a token and were not issued one can have a negative impact on a class. Manage these students by permitting them a cooling-off period (preferably away from the rest of the class). It is unwise to reinforce their angry and demanding behavior by issuing them a token just to calm them down. Consider making it a firm policy never to issue tokens if challenged for them.

Example of Guidelines for Caught You Doing the Right Thing *Contest*

1. *Teachers or other adults may give a token slip to any student who does the right thing.*

2. *Students are to put their names on their tokens as soon as possible after receiving them.*

3. *Students are responsible for keeping their tokens in a safe place.*

4. *Students will be disqualified from the contest for:*
   - *Arguing about whether or not they have earned a token.*
   - *Attempting to use someone else's tokens or making their own tokens.*

Variations on a Theme:

- Hold a *Caught You Doing the Right Thing* holiday contest. Distribute holiday-themed tokens and display them on a large holiday-themed chart. For example, distribute tokens in the shape of candy canes and have students attach their candy cane tokens (with their names written on them) on a large holiday tree chart or distribute tokens in the shape of pumpkins and have students attach their pumpkin tokens to a large cornucopia.

- With your principal's permission, involve the entire school in a *Caught You Doing the Right Thing* contest. Meet with interested faculty members to determine the student behaviors to be rewarded and the contest guidelines. Explain the guidelines to everyone, distribute tokens to all staff members, and initiate the contest.

- Give every student who earns at least a minimum number of tokens a nominal reward at the contest's conclusion (for example, a few extra minutes of recess, a small bag of M&Ms, or a small box of raisins).

Possible Rewards for
Caught You Doing the Right Thing
Contest Winners

- *Popcorn party*
- *Pizza party*
- *Watermelon party (outdoors with seedless melons)*
- *Viewing a special movie*
- *Lunch with teacher*
- *Outdoor picnic lunch with two friends*
- *One-on-one sports practice with teacher*
- *Homework pass (not good for long-term assignments)*
- *CD party (content of CDs previewed by teacher)*
- *Right Thing Rally with cheers and lots of noise*
- *Right Thing cookout*

Adult supervision must be available to monitor the contest winners (or the remainder of your class) during the special rewards activity. Provide this supervision by: soliciting parents to act as chaperones, placing a few of your students in several other teachers' classes during the reward time, or scheduling the reward party during your students' lunch period or during an elective class (with the permission of the administration, elective teacher, and reward winners' parents).

Compliment a Classmate Draw

It is midday and a class has just returned from lunch. The students are irritable and argumentative. After allowing them time to settle into the regular start of class routine, the teacher tells them to clear everything from their desks. She then says, "I think we need to spend a few minutes on Compliment a Classmate Draw.*"*

She distributes blank slips of paper to each student, directs them to write their name on their slip, fold it up, and place it in a small basket that she passes around the room. She places a list entitled, "Compliments We Can Give to Others" on the overhead projector and says, "Remember, when you draw a person's name you must give that person a sincere compliment. You can use the list on the overhead to help you. The complimented person then draws a name, gives that student a compliment, and justifies it. I'll start us off."

She takes a slip from the basket and says, "Our first complimentee is Tyree Monroe. Tyree, you are kind and helpful to others. I know this because just yesterday when Marsha dropped her books in the hallway you picked them up and handed them to her."

"Yeah, Tyree!" someone quips and several students giggle nervously.

The teacher smiles and holds the basket of name slips out to Tyree, "Okay, Tyree, it's your turn. Draw a name and give a compliment."

(What It Is:) *Compliment a Classmate Draw* is a morale-boosting motivational activity. It promotes a positive learning environment by building students' self esteem.

(Why It's Used:) Students who are self-absorbed and insensitive often create a negative learning environment by making unkind comments to others. *Compliment a Classmate Draw* helps create a positive learning environment by compelling students to contemplate and articulate their classmates' positive qualities.

(**How It's Done:**) Early in the school year hold a class discussion on the "golden rule," the importance of respecting the feelings of others, and the kinds of comments that make others feel good about themselves. Brainstorm a list of compliments that students might pay to one another (see List of Possible Compliments). Copy the list onto a transparency or save it to be used on a class computer display. (You might also direct your students to copy the list into their notebooks.) When students display insensitive behavior, make cruel comments to one another, are cranky and out of sorts, or just need a more positive view of things, introduce *Compliment a Classmate Draw* by placing the transparency on the overhead, and choosing students at random to give and receive valid compliments.

Sound Advice

List of Possible Compliments

Kind	Thoughtful	Generous
Hard-working	Serious	Religious
Optimistic	Honest	Friendly
Talented	Smart	Athletic
Graceful	Strong	Reliable
Happy	Funny	Pretty
Handsome	Well-dressed	Helpful
Determined	Caring	A good friend
A good musician	A good actor/actress	A good dancer
A good singer	A good writer	A good student

(**Perils and Pitfalls:**) On occasion, a student may refuse to compliment a classmate, even when presented with a list of compliments from which to choose. Prevent such an occurrence from escalating into an embarrassing put-down of the student who is to receive the compliment by quickly interceding on his or her behalf with a supportive comment spoken in incredulity such as, "Oh, I can't believe it! I see at least five compliments on the Compliment List that apply to Caitlin! Who sees one that easily fits Caitlin? Who sees another?"

Because young people are often unsure of how to behave when giving and receiving compliments, your students' initial reaction to the game may be feigned indifference or outright silliness. Overcome this conduct by modeling gracious behavior, patiently insisting that your students behave respectfully during this activity, and stressing that a simple "thank you" is the best way to respond to a compliment.

Also, since the time available for this activity is usually limited, not all students will have an opportunity to give or receive compliments. To insure that everyone has a chance to participate, retain the unselected name slips and draw from those names the next time you use *Compliment a Classmate Draw.*

Variations on a Theme:

- Have students give more than one compliment for each name drawn.

- Reverse the procedure by drawing compliments and identifying students whose behavior fits those compliments.

- Include teachers' names in the game, and should you use it on days when parents are visiting, include their names, too.

- Give a compliment from the teacher to each child in your class.

Compliment Their Character Composition

A class is ready to begin working on a writing assignment.

"All right, everyone," announces the teacher. "You know today's assignment is to write a composition complimenting a classmate's character. Before you're given the name of the person whose character you're going to describe, let's review the difference between a person's physical traits and his or her character traits. Who can explain the difference between the two for the class?"

"Well," responds a student, "physical traits are there for you to see, but character traits you have to conclude for yourself from the way the person behaves. Like we said before, a physical trait of a basketball star would be his height and you can see that, but his character trait might be kindness and you have to conclude that based on how he behaves. So physical traits have to do with appearance and character traits have to do with behavior."

"Excellent answer, Cherise!" says the teacher. She then calls up on the large class computer display screen a list of character traits compiled by the class in a previous lesson. "Your assignment for today," she continues, "is to write a composition about one of your classmates that describes that person's positive character traits. The person you are to write about will be assigned at random by drawing his or her name from a hat. Remember, before the period ends, you will share your composition with the person you wrote about so you want to stress that person's positive character traits. The purpose of this exercise is not only to sharpen our ability to observe the positive qualities in others, but also to inform them of our observations. When your classmate finishes reading the character compliment composition you have written about them, they should feel good about themselves."

(What It Is:) The *Compliment Their Character Composition* is a student self-esteem builder. It improves students' interpersonal relationships and increases students' pride in themselves.

Why It's Used: Older students sometimes put down their peers in an attempt to make themselves appear tough and intimidating. If not arrested, this behavior can have a negative impact on the learning environment. *Compliment Their Character Composition* encourages positive student communication and builds student self esteem.

How It's Done: Discuss with your students the importance of character and the difference between character traits and physical attributes. (Depending on the collective personality of your class, this discussion might parallel the one cited in the introductory scenario.) Once your students seem to understand the difference, work with them to develop a list of positive character traits and demonstrate how to use the information on the list as a reference when writing a *Compliment Their Character Composition*. As a class use a famous person as a model to write a *Compliment Their Character Composition*.

Sound Advice

Basic Character Trait Words

Thoughtful	Fair	Honest	Helpful
Friendly	Studious	Dependable	Intellectual
Diligent	Cooperative	Caring	Courteous
Pleasant	Empathetic	Gentle	Considerate
Generous	Organized	Loyal	Hard Working
Reliable	Agreeable	Careful	Sensible
Patient	Wise	Sensitive	Sincere
Trustworthy	Supportive	Ambitious	Inclusive

Perils and Pitfalls: Students who are unhappy with the random drawing-selection process or who aren't especially fond of the classmate whose name they draw may display their displeasure by making derogatory comments about their peers or refusing to work on the assignment. Such behavior is best managed by preemptive planning. Announce to the class that students may opt out of this assignment by instead writing a two- to three-page essay on a related topic such as the Meaning of Friendship, the Importance of Good Character, or the Importance of Community, but they must do so before they draw anyone's name.

Variations on a Theme:

- Assign this writing task monthly and have students compile a mini-booklet of all of the character compliments they receive.

- Have each student compile a list of his or her own character traits and write a *Compliment Their Character Composition* about him or herself.

Student of the Week

It is the start of a school day. Students have just completed the Pledge of Allegiance and are focused on their teacher.

"Before we begin the lesson, I need to announce our Student of the Week. This week's person is Steven Wilson," the teacher says. She holds up a large strip of tag board with Steven Wilson's name printed on it and tacks it to a colorful Student of the Week bulletin board display at the front of the room. Students seated near Steven Wilson give him modified high fives and he smiles sheepishly.

"Okay, guys," says the teacher. "It's time to start the lesson. Since our student of the week gets some extra privileges, Steve can start by taking the lunch order slip to the office."

What It Is: *Student of the Week* is a technique that enhances students' self esteem and feelings of self worth. It gives every child a chance to be treated specially and receive extra positive attention during the school year.

Why It's Used: *Student of the Week* helps create a positive and caring learning environment by providing each child, regardless of his or her academic ability or behavioral history, with a definite time to be accepted and honored.

How It's Done: Create a bulletin board to display the *Student of the Week's* name. Discuss the *Student of the Week* program with your class. Stress that students don't have to do anything special to be the *Student of the Week* (because they're already special). Explain that everyone in the class will have a chance to be the *Student of the Week* and that the *Student of the Week* will be given some extra privileges just for being the *Student of the Week*. Within the next few days, select a student and begin the program.

Perils and Pitfalls: Students are sometimes impatient for their turn to be *Student of the Week* and can be resentful of the student

Examples of Privileges for Student of the Week

- *Class messenger*
- *Team captain*
- *First in cafeteria line*
- *First in bus line*
- *Homework pass*
- *Wash boards*
- *Distribute and collect papers*
- *Distribute and collect books*
- *Clean-up captain*
- *Sit next to friend for a day*
- *Lunch with the teacher*
- *Help mark papers*
- *Lunch in the classroom with two or three friends (with adult supervision)*
- *Get to wear a special Student of the Week hat or T-shirt (see Variations on a Theme).*

whose week it is. Students are sometimes impatient for their turn to be *Student of the Week* and can be resentful of the student whose week it is. Manage these normal human reactions by stressing that everyone will have their week and when they do, they will want their classmates to be glad for them and treat them kindly. It is essential to your students' feelings of worthiness and your credibility that, once you begin a *Student of the Week* program, you continue it until every child has at least one opportunity to be a Student of the Week.

Occasionally, when the *Student of the Week* has serious behavioral problems, he or she will behave arrogantly and irresponsibly throughout their week. Manage such situations by carefully choosing the special privileges given to this child and carefully monitoring his or her actions throughout the week. Should you have many students with behavioral problems, consider modifying the program from *Student of the Week* to *Student of the Day*.

Variations on a Theme:

- Take a photo of the *Student of the Week* (digital or Polaroid) and use it as part of your *Student of the Week* display. Sign and date it and give it to the *Student of the Week* as a memento. (Be aware of your school district's policy on taking and using students' pictures before using this variation.)

- Acquire a T-shirt with the words *Student of the Week* printed on it. (Choose a size large enough to fit over your students' normal school clothing.) Allow the *Student of the Week* to wear the shirt throughout his or her week.

- Allow the *Student of the Week* to add some of his or her photos and mementos to the *Student of the Week* bulletin board display. Provide a small block of time at the end of the week for the student to talk about what he or she brought and why it is important.

Silence is Bliss

A teacher is working in her classroom when the principal arrives at her door. "Ms. Alston, I hate to infringe on your planning time, but there is an emergency and we need your help. Mr. Seekford is very ill and has left for the day. A substitute is on the way, but she won't arrive for at least twenty minutes and we need someone to cover for Bill. Could you possibly help us out?"

"Okay, but I can only cover until 10:30 when my next class starts," Ms. Alston agrees hesitantly. She knows that Mr. Seekford's class is often poorly behaved and she is not looking forward to dealing with them.

As she enters Mr. Seekford's room the noise level is deafening. She scans the room, sees a handful of students who appear to be completing the work assigned to them, and places a sheet of blank paper on each of their desks. She ignores the comments of a boisterous student who says, "Hey, substitute lady, I didn't get a paper!"

After a few minutes, Ms. Alston glances at her watch, returns to the students who are working appropriately, and places her initials on the blank sheets of paper she previously placed on their desks. Several talkative students notice that the substitute has given each of their quieter and more focused peers a piece of paper and that she is writing something on it every few minutes. They stop talking for a bit to try to determine what is happening. When they do, Ms. Alston gives each of them a blank sheet of paper. She points to the assignment sheet on their desks, and as soon as they glance over it, she initials their blank sheets.

Once the more focused students have accumulated several sets of initials on their teacher-distributed sheets and the large majority of the class is settled and working, Ms. Alston announces, "It's good to see so many of Mr. Seekford's students following directions and working independently. I'm sure Mr. Seekford will be pleased and will want to reward those who worked the hardest. In the meantime, let's see how many initials this class can collect for working well during the time I'm here."

(**What It Is:**) *Silence is Bliss* is a low-key behavior modification procedure. It quietly focuses on and gives tangible teacher attention to students who exhibit desirable behavior instead of loudly denouncing and giving teacher attention to students who exhibit undesirable behavior.

(**Why It's Used:**) *Silence is Bliss* is used to calm a group of students who are so noisy and chaotic that the teacher cannot gain their attention decorously.

(**How It's Done:**) Stay calm and resolve to be patient. Quietly observe everyone's behavior and quickly give blank sheets of paper with your initials on them only to those students who are behaving appropriately. (You may have to begin by accepting somewhat marginal behavior as appropriate.) As you give the initialed sheets to students, softly compliment them on their appropriate behavior. You might say for example, "It's nice to see you following directions and completing your assignment. I know your teacher will be pleased when I tell him." As these students continue working, tangibly reinforce their appropriate behavior by randomly initialing their sheets. As other students become concerned that they are missing out on something and begin to behave more appropriately, distribute an initialed sheet to each of them. Continue initialing sheets at random intervals as more and more students follow through and focus on the tasks at hand.

(**Perils and Pitfalls:**) This technique is ineffective when students are out of their seats and milling about. Under such circumstances you must first direct students to take their seats and as they do so, immediately reinforce their compliance through the distribution and use of the initialed sheets.

If you are familiar with behavior modification techniques, you might choose to distribute some type of token as reinforcement in lieu of teacher-initialed reinforcement sheets. However, token reinforcers work well only when clear guidelines are in place regarding their handling, otherwise, they can become flying projectiles, pilfered objects, or a disinterested student's creative building project.

Also, issuing any type of tangible reinforcer, from writing your initials on a sheet of paper to distributing M&Ms, can cause students who do not receive a reinforcer to complain vociferously that you have overlooked their exemplary behavior. This type of student complaint is difficult to manage, since if you acknowledge that you have indeed overlooked a student and give him a reinforcer, you will be inundated with similar complaints from poorly behaved student con-artists. Therefore, ninety-nine times out of one hundred, it's best to address complaints of unfairness by steadfastly refusing to address them.

Variations on a Theme:

- Once you have distributed a few blank sheets to students and others are beginning to realize something unusual is taking place, lock them in by writing something cryptic on the board that hints at a possible reward (for example, extra recess or homework pass).

Tennis, Anyone?

Students in a seventh-grade classroom are moving their desks so they can work in groups of six. Although the room is spacious and has a hard surfaced floor, the transition is taking place without the ear-splitting scraping and screeching that normally accompanies such moves. A closer look at the classroom furniture explains why. The feet on each student's desk and chair are encased in tennis balls.

(What It Is:) *Tennis, Anyone?* is a noise-reducing technique. It creates an adaptable learning environment that is more tolerable and conducive to learning.

(Why It's Used:) Rearranging student seating to address a variety of activities is an effective teaching strategy; however, the noise created by such moves is often disruptive and counter productive. Tennis ball furniture shoes stop the noise and creates a more peaceful classroom.

(How It's Done:) Collect a large quantity of used tennis balls— tennis clubs, YMCAs, and colleges are usually willing to donate their threadbare discards to needy teachers. Cut a small x in one side of each tennis ball just large enough to allow the foot of a desk or chair to fit through. (Take care not to cut yourself when doing this.) Slip the tennis ball over a desk foot and repeat the procedure until all student desks and chairs are properly shod.

(Perils and Pitfalls:) Collecting, preparing, and installing the tennis ball shoes is time consuming. Recruit parent volunteers, teaching colleagues, teaching assistants, and student teachers to help with these tasks. Because desk chairs with feet encased in tennis ball shoes slide easily they can be somewhat risky to students who have the dangerous habit of rocking back in their chairs, leaving only the back feet on the floor. Remind these students of how unsafe their "rocking habit" is (with or without tennis ball furniture shoes), insist that they refrain from rocking in your classroom, and be sure to inform their parents of your concern regarding their children's unsafe behavior and your efforts to correct it.

(**Variations on a Theme:**)

- When working with older students, in lieu of putting tennis ball shoes on every desk and chair, put them only on the furniture of students who take perverse pleasure in creating ear-splitting furniture moving din. Often these deliberate noise mongers will not appreciate having tennis ball shoes placed only on their furniture and willingly make noiseless moves once the shoes are removed.

Sound Advice

Tennis, Anyone?
Seating Arrangements, and the Best Possible Learning Environment

While tennis ball shoes help reduce noise as student seating is rearranged, the overall arrangement affects classroom noise levels and lesson objectives by encouraging or discouraging student interaction.

Separating desks into solitary entities can insure student integrity during testing and reduce student interactions throughout a lesson. Placing desks in groups of four or six to form square or rectangular tables can encourage student interaction and discussion. Arranging all of the desks in a room to form one large circle can promote a whole class discussion, while arranging them into separate rows or columns that face the main teaching area can increase student attention and diminish student interaction.

There are, of course, many other seating configurations that can be used in classrooms. (The New Teacher's Handbook offers more comprehensive information about different seating arrangements and the effect they have on student interactions.) However, it's important that you select those used during a lesson that best meet your students' needs and the lesson's objectives in order to create the best possible learning environment.

Guess That Student

It is near the end of the school day on a Friday. The last lesson for the week has ended. Students are packed up and ready to leave for the weekend. Suddenly an announcement comes over the public address system, "Boys and girls, teachers and staff, due to a traffic accident nearby our school, the buses have not yet arrived and today's dismissal will be delayed several minutes."

The students begin grumbling their disappointment when the teacher stops them. "Okay, guys, since we have to stay a little longer, let's do Guess That Student. *I'll start us off. See if you can guess whom in this class I'm describing. This person is right-handed, has brown eyes, plays the piano, takes ballet lessons, is reading* Tuck Everlasting, *has a good sense of humor, and hardly ever misses a day of school."*

Immediately several students raise their hands. "I guess I made my clues to the mystery student too easy," she says as she calls on a student seated toward the back of the room. "Yes, Terrell, who do you think the mystery student is?"

"I think it's Staci Howe," answers Terrell, "'cause she's the only one in the class who matches all of the clues."

"What do you think, Staci?" asks the teacher. "Do you think Terrell is correct?"

"Yes, I do," answers Staci with a smile.

"Well, so do I," says the teacher. "Okay, Terrell it's your turn to choose a mystery student and see if we can guess who it is from the clues you give us."

(What It Is:) *Guess That Student* is an enjoyable deductive reasoning activity. It focuses student attention, strengthens their deductive reasoning skills, and helps them see the positive views others have of them.

Why It's Used: Sometimes circumstances beyond a teacher's control result in students having too much down time with its subsequent less-than-acceptable behavior. *Guess That Student* fills these instructional voids with an enjoyable teacher-directed deductive reasoning activity.

How It's Done: Explain *Guess That Student* to your students and model its use for them. (Review the introductory section above.) Employ *Guess That Student* whenever circumstances dictate.

Perils and Pitfalls: Problems can arise if students use negatives to describe their mystery person. Warn the class before beginning that such comments will not be tolerated and immediately stop any student who attempts to use them.

Also, students sometimes make their best friends in the class their mystery persons, fooling no one and creating simpering silliness. To avoid this, strongly suggest that students not choose their best friends to be their mystery person and stress that clues should be somewhat challenging.

Variations on a Theme:

- Have students use only specific descriptors as clues (for example: The mystery person's likes and dislikes, favorite foods, or character traits).